The Objects of Experience

The Objects of Experience

Transforming Visitor-Object Encounters in Museums

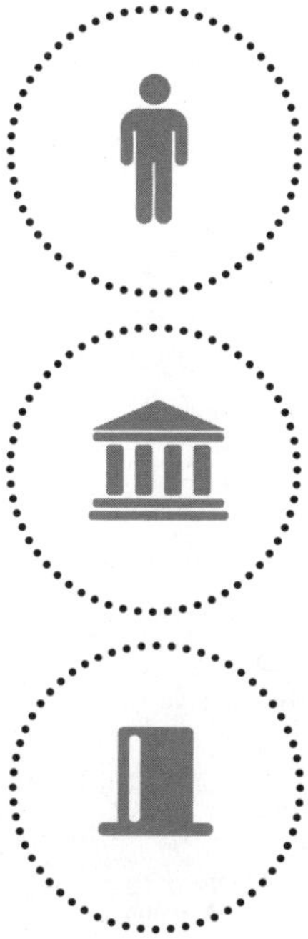

Elizabeth Wood and Kiersten F. Latham

Left Coast Press Inc.

WALNUT CREEK, CA

Left Coast Press, Inc. is committed to preserving ancient forests and natural resources. We elected to print this title on 30% post consumer recycled paper, processed chlorine free. As a result, for this printing, we have saved:

3 Trees (40' tall and 6-8" diameter)
1 Million BTUs of Total Energy
228 Pounds of Greenhouse Gases
1,238 Gallons of Wastewater
83 Pounds of Solid Waste

Left Coast Press, Inc. made this paper choice because our printer, Thomson-Shore, Inc., is a member of Green Press Initiative, a nonprofit program dedicated to supporting authors, publishers, and suppliers in their efforts to reduce their use of fiber obtained from endangered forests.

For more information, visit www.greenpressinitiative.org

Environmental impact estimates were made using the Environmental Defense Paper Calculator. For more information visit: www.papercalculator.org.

Left Coast Press, Inc.
1630 North Main Street, #400
Walnut Creek, CA 94596
www.LCoastPress.com

ISBN 978-1-61132-213-8 hardcover
ISBN 978-1-61132-214-6 paperback
ISBN 978-1-61132-215-4 institutional eBook
ISBN 978-1-61132-652-4 consumer eBook

Library of Congress Cataloging-in-Publication Data
Wood, Elizabeth E.
The objects of experience : transforming visitor-object encounters in museums / Elizabeth Wood, Kiersten F Latham.
pages cm
Includes bibliographical references and index.
ISBN 978-1-61132-213-2 (hardback) -- ISBN 978-1-61132-214-9 (paperback) --
ISBN 978-1-61132-215-6 (institutional ebook) --ISBN 978-1-61132-652-4 (consumer eBook)
1. Museum exhibits--Psychological aspects. 2. Museum techniques. I. Latham, Kiersten Fourshé. II. Title.
AM151.W66 2013
069.5--dc23
2013025287

Printed in the United States of America

∞ ™ The paper used in this publication meets the minimum requirements of American National Standard for Information Sciences—Permanence of Paper for Printed Library Materials, ANSI/NISO Z39.48–1992.

Book design by Devenish Design
Cover design by Hannah Jennings

Contents

Illustrations

FIGURES

TABLES

Acknowledgments

For Erik, Mark, and Callan

We gratefully acknowledge the support and contributions from all the students, colleagues, and museum professionals who have aided in our efforts. We find inspiration in collaborative work, and everyone's contribution made a difference in some way.

In particular we'd like to express gratitude to the many museum professionals who shared their experiences and thoughts on exhibits and programs: Carter Lupton, Dawn Scher Thomae, Al Muchka, Claudia Jacobson, Dawn Koceja, Gaye-Lynn Clyde, Allen Young, Jim Kelly, Sue Borkin, Art Montgomery, and Ellen Censky at the Milwaukee Public Museum; Felicia Katz-Harris at the Museum of International Folk Art; Ava Ferguson at Monterey Bay Aquarium; Greg Hardison and Mike Deetsch at the Kentucky Historical Society; and Sharon Dean, Angela O'Neal, and Jason Crabill at the Ohio Historical Society. Special thanks to the following staff at The Children's Museum of Indianapolis for participating in test sessions and testing activities: Charity Counts, Chris Carron, Melissa Pederson, Ned Shaw, Tricia O'Connor, Laura Ferries, Jennifer Leach, Despi Ross, Cathy Donnelly, Cathy Hamaker, Josh Estes, Monica Humphrey, Carey Meier, Rachael Mathews, Janna Bennett, Tris Perkins, Jennifer Pace-Robinson, and Barbara Wolf.

Thank you to Dolly Hayde, Erin Hetrick, Claire Thoma, Cathy Hamaker, Abby Wolf, Donna Braden, John Simmons, Erik Peterson, and our anonymous reviewers for thoughtful and probing discussions of our work. In addition thank you to Emily Wicks for her help managing all of our references and examples. And finally, to John Gouin for making our graphics beautiful.

A special thank you to: Stefanie Clark for use of her essay on Ere Ibeji; Jay, Alicia and Samantha Scribner and the rest of the Scribner family; Hurricane Sandy; Jennifer, Mitch, and Stefania at Left Coast Press, Inc.

This project was partially supported by Indiana University's New Frontiers in the Arts & Humanities Program, the IUPUI Arts and Humanities Institute, and the IUPUI Museum Studies program. Support was also provided by Kent State School of Library and Information Science and the College of Communication and Information.

Introduction

This is a book for thinking about the objects and experiences that constitute the basic elements of museum work. The best museums are living, breathing places where exhibitions and programs bring important *things* to life. That they create places for the meaningful exchange of ideas between visitors and objects is one of the marvels of what museums do. As museums strive to bring visitors into the center of their work, museum practitioners must study the experience of visitors being in a space with the things that constitute the world around us. This book will provide new ways for museum practitioners to think about and use *objects* as a way to connect with visitors.

The work is specifically about the encounters between visitors *and* objects in museum settings. Museums are institutions dedicated to the acquisition and preservation of the objects of human existence, whether they have formal collections or not. They develop collections in order to care for, maintain, protect, study, show off, share, tout, reveal, educate, and otherwise continue the story of humanity through history, art, and science. Objects are important to humans. The world is comprised of and shaped by human interaction with objects; it includes human contact with things seen and unseen, memorable and forgettable, extraordinary and mundane. These objects often symbolize significant community or local meaning, the great cultural wonders of the world, and provide witness to human aesthetic achievements. At the same time, each museum visitor's encounter with an object on display has its own significance to that individual. The union of people's experiences and the unique characteristics of objects forms the foundation of something far greater than the sum of its parts. These elements of personal object experience ultimately shape people's meaning making in museums and other informal learning environments.

Elizabeth Wood and Kiersten F. Latham, "Introduction" in *The Objects of Experience: Transforming Visitor-Object Encounters in Museums*, pp 9-21.

Defining Objects

Throughout the book we intentionally use the term *object* rather than *artifact* or *specimen*, and this use is intentionally broad to mean any physical, tangible *thing* that is part of the museum experience. All museums, whether they have a collection or not, are composed of and use objects. These include historic artifacts, documents, natural specimens, works of art, and all the other items found in a museum's collection. But these things also include hands-on objects, props, benches, exhibit furniture, cabinets, walls, and so on. Each *thing* in a museum represents some aspect of the human or natural world. This intentional choice to think about *objects* rather than artifacts is a way to expand the range of physical things that practitioners can study in museum settings. This helps museum professionals from all areas of practice break out of older models that may limit the understanding of potential interactions with objects.

The study of human interaction with objects is not new; in fact, many fields of study have different opinions and perspectives on what objects mean to people. Early knowledge of and about objects in museums drew from the fields of material culture studies or anthropology, and these studies emphasized human uses of, or practices with objects. In art museums, an object (i.e. a work of art) might be understood through the study of its aesthetic and/or historical importance. In a natural history museum, an object might represent a "type specimen," studied particularly for its defining features of an organism. Through these orientations the role of the object was thought of as part of the "text" or "script" of a museum exhibition that visitors might "read." This view of objects and artifacts as text presumed that the object served as a specific representation of an idea, or expected a certain level of disciplinary knowledge (see Schlereth, 1992). To this mix we add a new orientation through the idea of a lived experience of objects that shapes a visitor's understanding toward more individual and personal meaning.

The Role of Objects in People's Lives

What would people be without objects? The world is and has been entirely shaped by interactions with the physical, three-dimensional things that encompass the human environment. Each object takes on a different significance for every person depending on where or how she or he encounters it. Similarly, objects are the lifeblood of museums. They are the basis for most of the work that museums do, whether it is in maintaining a collection or shaping a visitor's educational experience. Museums *can* exist without collections of artifacts or specimens; they cannot exist without objects. There are plenty of places—whether called a museum, a science center, an interpretive center, zoo, aquarium, botanical garden—that thrive without formal, specific collections. It is not the collection per se that makes a museum or museum-like experience: it is, rather, the act of *bringing together* people and objects.

Rather than worrying about what constitutes a true museum artifact, our concern is how museums understand objects and what museums do with those objects in order to support visitor learning and experience. What does it mean to *know* an object? How do people *experience* the world through objects? How can objects *reveal* the world we live in? These are not new questions: philosophers have asked them for centuries. As researchers of human experience with objects, and with many years of museum experience in the areas of education, curation, collections management, and exhibit development, we think these are the questions that museum staff need to be asking too.

Meaning and Objects

One of the most challenging issues in thinking about the role of objects in museums, and in general, is that in the big picture, the essential meaning and significance of any object is fundamentally unfixed (Heidegger, 1967; Hodder, 1986; Hooper-Greenhill, 2000; Olsen, 2010; Pearce, 1990, 1994). This means that when a visitor encounters an object, the meaning that the person creates is part of his or her own particular, unique understanding of the experience. The changing properties of an object rely on the context in which a person uses it and depend on their relationship and identity with it. Consider for a moment a house or apartment you lived in as a child. All of the nooks and crannies, the rooms, and the features of that dwelling have a particular meaning based on what it was like to live there as a result of the experiences you had. The meaning of the house is much more than simply describing and defining those features, or in providing facts or impressions. Instead the meaning is derived from our attachments, memories, and experiences with that house—its essence.

The essence of an object, then, is incomplete without a self—an individual—and the time to draw out the sometimes hidden reality of the object and what it means. There are countless ways in which a person encounters objects in the world. In each instance the intersection between self and object is mediated by all manner of information that a person brings with them as well as all the potential meanings that objects can have. A wonderful example of how this personal connection works in a museum setting is in the guided tours at the Lower Eastside Tenement Museum in New York. As visitors enter the building, they stand briefly in the entryway at the foot of a large staircase. The guide invites visitors to "touch the banister that every person in this house used at some point in time." Although it is unlikely that these visitors ever lived in this particular building, the act of touching the banister and imagining those who lived there evokes a kind of personal connection that can reach farther than a simple description.

The many layers of a person's life and experience contribute to different ways of knowing and being in the world. The more connections one has with objects, the more uniquely meaningful and important those layers of life become. When something is precious to us, we know it inside and out (Bachelard, 1968; Marcoux, 2001). We can intimately describe its features, and we know when it changes or is replaced. Museum objects can be like this for visitors. Staff who know how to unlock the key aspects of the encounter with an object can enhance the visitors' ability to make meaning from that experience.

There is no question that objects are important features of museums. Consider for a moment a typical display in a history museum, art museum, or natural history museum. A small label might identify the title or type of artifact, or give details such as an accession number, donor information, date of creation, material composition, etc. A text label providing background information on the object will probably tell the reader about its origins, uses, history, or owners. Whether displayed in a case, on a pedestal, or perhaps in a diorama, the traditional exhibition focuses on the material and cultural qualities of the object itself. This approach de-emphasizes a personal or emotional connection between visitor and object. Imagine coming across a teddy bear in an exhibit about childhood toys where the label simply says, "The Teddy Bear, named after President Teddy Roosevelt, has been popular since its induction in 1903." Where does your mind go when you see this teddy bear? We all know that there's more to this teddy bear than its namesake. Moving beyond the basic information helps visitors connect on an individual level.

For some visitors, especially if they lack prior knowledge to draw from, the object is experienced from across a divide of meaning. For others, such as a professional, expert or amateur enthusiast, an interaction with the object might reinforce a personal interest, or perhaps present new or important information to add to their prior knowledge. The *Mitohseenionki (The People's Place)* gallery at the Eiteljorg Museum in Indianapolis, Indiana, tells stories of Native American tribes from Indiana using multiple perspectives. The exhibit design focuses on two circular pathways. The inside circle incorporates the Native American curator's voice along with contributions from other Native American members of the design team to describe the experiences of Indiana heritage and traditions. Traditional and contemporary objects mixed together in cases help demonstrate the permanence of Native culture. On the outside circle of the exhibit, labels and historic information from majority cultures give additional context to the Native American perspective. The combined stories and voices enable visitors to build on their knowledge and hear personal connections that might not otherwise be told.

These same personal connections happen outside the museum setting too. The encounters that people have with everyday objects can be exceptional avenues to deep meaning making and thinking about the world. All kinds of people are able to draw on a wide range of personal interests, professional knowledge, or life history when making sense of objects. In fact, the human experience with objects is so ubiquitous that people often take it for granted. Yet, people understand and explore the world through countless experiences and interactions with physical things. Each of these encounters can translate, mediate, or inform meaning that people make in the world.

In the museum setting, greater attention to the visitor's experience with objects can reinvigorate the meaning, value, and relevance of the museum as a whole. We who work in museums need to acknowledge that experience and meaning making in the museum do not occur without objects. Rather, objects are the *basis of the visitor experience.*

Moving Toward New Museum Structures

The role of museum collections, the place and prominence of objects, and the use of objects in exhibitions and programs is changing (Gurian, 2006; Hein, 2000; Roberts, 1997). Collections are no longer necessarily the most prominent features of many museum experiences, nor do they mean the same to any one person or group of people. Even at present, a multitude of museum professionals—from exhibition developers and designers, to educators and collections managers, to scholars of museum studies—continue to ponder and debate the relevance and meaning of museums and their collections. This kind of dialogue on objects provides opportunities to rethink and reimagine the world of objects within the visitor experience.

As museums move toward more and more visitor-centered experiences, their staffs need to think carefully about the roles that objects play in creating those interactions. What functions are objects supposed to perform in museums, and how do museums' structures contribute to that work? For the last hundred years (and more) the traditional organization of objects in a museum has been hierarchical (Conn, 1998; Hein, 2000). It consisted of a top-down structure of access and management characterized by functionally separated staff, and this separation divided the work of the museum into discrete tasks and responsibilities, making overlaps between staff knowledge rare. Eventually this divide led to placing collections objects under the purview of single departments, rather than sharing them among the entire museum staff. This structure slowly led to a museum in which the object became a secondary aspect of certain elements of museum practice rather than a focal point for all aspects of museum functions.

In this traditional system, only those museum staff who directly deal with the collection have a strong connection to and intimate knowledge of the objects. For visitors, much less most of the museum staff, the exact contents of a museum's collection can be a mystery—only unlocked by the curator or collection manager. Already this lack of connection, emotionally and/or intellectually, can create a barrier for staff knowing the power of using objects in the museum. Further, the training that different staff have around the purpose and intention of a museum's collections, exhibitions, or programs can exacerbate these mysteries; the difficulty for each staff member lies hidden in the subtext and knowledge from his or her perspective. Museum educators and exhibit developers base their projects around the available content and objects with a particular goal of learning and interaction. The curator has a deep knowledge of the content and history of an object along with a perspective of that object within a broader field of study. The collection manager, who has learned classification schemes and knows the standardized terminology used in collections databases, works with the objects through these classifications. The curator, educator, and collection manager must also work with the museum's standardized catalogue entries, even though these might not always have sufficient information to reflect possible visitor experiences with objects.

Intentionally or not, the hierarchical system of object classification erects barriers to "outsiders" who want to use them. Certainly there are communication problems across different roles within the museum that inhibit discussion on collections. It may be that different kinds of staff speak different and not mutually intelligible "languages" of practice. And, perhaps worse, none of these perspectives may correspond to the visitor's curiosities. For example, the current entry for puppets in *Nomenclature for Museum Cataloging 3.0* (Bourcier & Rogers, 2010) lists seven different types of puppets and classifies the objects as "Public Entertainment Devices." An exhibition developer is likely working with a very different technical terminology than the collection manager, and may even be operating from a wholly different concept of puppets. Many of us, after all, think about a puppet as a storytelling device, rather than as device made of papier-mâché and fabric. Every specialization uses unique language and orientation that is distinctive from public work, but ultimately both curator and collection manager need to find a way to represent the reality of people's experiences of those objects.

The challenge with this traditional system of object organization in museums is that it limits the potential for all museum staff to make the best use of the human element in helping visitors relate to objects. This limitation started to become obvious as more and more museums found that their exhibits lacked relevance or connection to their visitors (Hood, 2004). The shifting perspectives around visitors, both inside and outside the museum field, reflected a significant change in the way that people expect to interact with information. In short, the collective view of *knowledge* in the world at large underwent a major change: modern society is increasingly dependent on digital experiences and expects quick, on-demand information at any time and anywhere. Many museums' ways of thinking about knowledge have, as a result, shifted from worrying about what is in their collections to how the visitor will experience the messages and content of the exhibitions (Falk & Dierking, 1992; McLean, 1993; Serrell, 1996).

Museums were founded on the premise of discrete disciplines like history, anthropology, archaeology, and art, and along the way the emphasis on discipline-specific knowledge started to create barriers for visitors. For the most part, the typical label texts accompanying an exhibition's objects have been more about describing human identity, goals, or experiences, rather than providing ways for the visitor to connect those objects personally. For example, a typical cultural history display dating from the mid-1960s, "Dance and Belief," depicts two figures clothed in ritual garb and

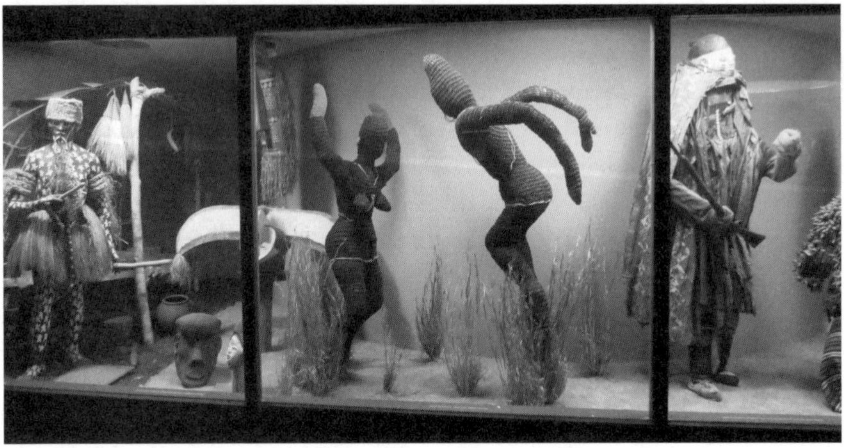

FIGURE I.1 A more traditional museum display of objects. Photo by Elee Wood.

dramatically positioned as if in the middle of a dance (Figure I.1). The text accompanying the exhibit simply states, "Boy and girl initiates of a sacred society. Mabila. (Cameroon)" (American Museum of Natural History, 2012). Nearby in a similar display of figures, a text panel of approximately 300 words explains the coming of age ritual for the Bira people. Most of the text explains the process of the initiation and describes the objects in the case, but it is not entirely clear how the text connects to the various figures. While visitors may appreciate the sense of energy and rhythm evoked by the objects, the display gives them few other ways to personally connect with the dancers. This type of exhibitry and interpretation places the objects in a distant, and even inaccessible, setting. Although the dynamic visual elements may capture the visitor's attention, the label text does little to keep the visitor connected or interested in what they are seeing.

Is the Object Experience?

The recent rise in social networking that has contributed to new ways of thinking about the world also fostered the realization that the collections-centered operation of museums might not be as successful in the current social environment. The introduction of the World Wide Web in the mid-1990s reflected a new era of connectivity and interaction in society. Initially, the Web provided people innovation through "hypermedia" and the ability to "link" to information across a wide array of sources. By the early 2000s the idea of Web 2.0, or social networking, launched new models for individual people to contribute to the development of innumerable ideas and projects. Across multiple aspects of life, the revolution of social connection and interactivity gave people the ability to more easily build interconnected systems of information and relationships. In the museum, the idea of interconnectivity and interaction encouraged a greater emphasis on visitor experience. Visitors began demanding more control of their own experiences, and museums often gave it.

To an extent, this change resulted in a wide range of attitudes (and arguments) around what makes a "museum." Museums suddenly began moving away from a collections-centered identity, to one that acknowledged the potential for museums about concepts, or for specific audiences and purposes—effectively reflecting the growing trend toward the social network. Noted museum scholar Elaine Gurian suggested to the field that the role of the museum is in "the ownership of the story, rather than the object itself" (Gurian, 2006, p.35). Many other museum scholars have also recently surmised that it is not objects themselves that the museum field should understand, but rather the treatment, display, use, and interpretation of objects that need better development. For example, Conn (2010) writes, "objects have lost pride of place in many museums because they aren't necessary to fulfill some of the functions people now expect museums to perform" (p. 22). Those functions, according to Conn, include providing more opportunities that respond to the needs of museum visitors such as interactive or hands-on experiences, greater diversity of content, or more accessible content. The focus of recent publications on objects or about collections ranges from the idea of *touch* as a powerful interaction (Pye, 2007) to materiality and the notions of embodied experiences with objects (Dudley, 2010) to use of museum objects in health care (Chatterjee, MacDonald, Prytherch, & Noble, 2008) to the collections themselves (Caple, 2006) and, most broadly, to theories and ideas on objects (Candlin & Guins, 2009).

The notion that story and experience should take precedence over the supremacy of the object delivers both good news and bad news for museums. The positive is that the museum staff can heighten their awareness of visitors' role and experience within the museum. The negative is that with the emphasis on visitor experience as paramount, use of the objects in supporting those experiences got lost. The dialogue around the role and purpose of museums and visitor experiences provides opportunities to rethink and reimagine the world of objects in shaping the visitor experience. Greater attention to the role of objects as central to the museum visit can provide an increased level of accessibility to content and collections.

A system of sharing ideas, telling stories, making connections, and generating new content suggests the idea of a "networked" museum. This concept signals a museum where experiences or ideas move back and forth in a system that lives and breathes through staff and visitor relationships that are developed across, around, and through objects. In a networked museum model, the objects—all of the things of the museum—anchor the webs of information and people across all aspects of museum work. This new system represents a move away from the traditional, collection-centered museum, to the person/object-centered museum, where objects serve as mediators for a wide range of collaborations between the visitor, the exhibition designers and developers, the collections managers, curators, marketers, educators and so on. The networked museum is the one that will translate, build, and create stories through meaningful experiences with objects.

An Overview of The Objects of Experience

What if museum staff thought about, and planned to connect their visitors intellectually and emotionally with collections in the same way that people connect to everyday objects? What if museums sought a way to harness the visitor's potential to make a personal connection with museum objects? By looking at and thinking about objects in a different manner, museum staff can transform the experiences of many visitors who walk through their museum's doors each day. Rather than seeing objects in a collection as the sole reason for experiences in the museum, and instead of holding experiences as the sole organizer of museum visits, the goal for staff would be to place the object *and* experience of that object into a new, networked context.

The *Object Knowledge Framework* presented in this book provides that new context. It is an interdisciplinary framework for using objects to connect museum visitors to themselves, to others, and to their world. The experience of object knowledge is not about separating the object from the subject, but instead is about the potential for shared connection between people and objects.

Creating the Framework for Visitor-Object Experiences

Section One, *Thinking about Objects,* outlines the major concepts discussed in this book and examines the ways in which objects—specifically in museums and informal learning settings—contribute to the human experience and how human interactions with objects can benefit the overall museum experience. In Chapter One, *Object Knowledge,* we present guiding concepts of the Object Knowledge Framework to think about the ways that a person's life experiences and viewpoints shape the way that they take in the information about an object. This includes an overview of our integrated phenomenological perspective of objects, presenting the basic concepts that guide an understanding of the lived experience of objects. It also involves an examination of the ways that people "know" objects not only through cultural connotations and physical qualities but also through familiarity. This discussion of the interrelated nature of the individual, group, and material meaning of objects provides the backdrop for thinking about the role of objects and collections in museum exhibitions.

Chapter Two, *The Object Knowledge Framework,* presents in-depth background on our development of the Framework. Drawing on multiple fields of study, the ideas presented here offer readers an interdisciplinary view on contemporary definitions of object knowledge—the meaning of objects in people's lives, the role of objects within a museum setting, and the cultural significance that museum practitioners create through exhibitions and interactions with the material world. This chapter outlines the definition of objects across a vast array of disciplines and demonstrates how these ideas fit into the Framework. This eclectic mixing of theory and philosophy creates a unique and innovative view of objects that is more specific to the museum field than any one discipline on its own.

The Importance of Individual Encounters with Objects

What kind of experiences can objects evoke? The idea that objects have meaning and power raises awareness of the transformative nature of visitor-object experiences. What matters most in these moments are the ways in which the person encounters the object. By focusing on the visitor's transaction with objects, museums can begin to think differently about the stories and information that come with different objects. They might start by asking, "What role and purpose did any of these objects serve for their owners? Why do they end up in a museum? What do these objects say to our current visitors?" The answers to these questions help demonstrate the importance of museum objects and the sense they might make to museum visitors. The value of using this approach lies in understanding the human-object relationship and why objects matter to people. Taking a closer look at the meanings people ascribe to objects, whether in museums or not, reveals the fundamental role that objects serve in our lives, and can, perhaps, reignite a deeper way of looking and knowing what is in the world around us.

Objects in the world, whether they are part of day-to-day activities or something special like in a museum, offer people ways in which they can explore and make meaning. Encounters with objects can stimulate or represent experiences that facilitate personal growth and development, an essential component of learning. The Object Knowledge Framework demonstrates how a person brings different dimensions of individual experiences to any object encounter. Similarly, the object itself has a range of qualities and factual information that establish its presence. This information contributes to the way a person encounters it. When a person encounters an object and mixes information about the object with his or her own life experiences and perspectives, powerful sensory, emotional and/or intellectual awareness can occur for the visitor.

New Research on Personal Connections to Objects

Section Two, *Object Relationships,* traces the evocative and provocative nature of the personal relationship with objects through three different research studies that highlight aspects of the Object Knowledge Framework. By exploring different ways of experiencing objects, readers will come to see how memory, meaning, and transformation can come from deep and meaningful object interactions that occur both inside and outside of museum settings. Included are narrative examples on the meanings that individuals derived of a variety of childhood objects, everyday objects, and museum objects. This section elaborates on the ways in which these objects generate a sense of identity for the person, aid in the individual's relation to other people, and provide avenues for further exploration of ideas and experiences. The goal of the chapters in this section is to capture some of the key meanings that people attribute to objects in a variety of encounters and to explore how objects support identity, stimulate revelation, and evoke a sense of reverence in people's lived experience.

Chapter Three, *Objects as Identity* presents an investigation of everyday objects saved from childhood that play a meaningful role in people's adult lives and explores personal stories of museum objects from a similar perspective. Chapter Four, *Objects as Memories,* examines an informal family museum, a place that is not quite a personal collection and not quite a full-fledged museum. Here we look at the way multiple people can have different experiences with a collection of objects and how display practices can stimulate memories. Finally, Chapter Five, *Objects as Reverence,* explores the idea of "numinous" experiences in museums and demonstrates the power that these objects have for visitors, once the objects become an integral part of museum experience.

New Directions for Museum Practice

What does a meaningful visitor-object encounter look like? How does it work? People rarely just encounter an object and immediately have a life-changing moment. They need a process of reflection, or a way to develop curiosity and interest in order to highlight the meaning the object can provide. Section Three, *Object Transformations,* takes a practical look at strategies to transform the visitor-object experience in museums. These approaches stimulate thinking, learning, and personal development through museum exhibitions and other informal learning experiences. Included are practical suggestions that focus on elements of design, orientations to exhibition themes, messages, and content as avenues to increase visitor learning. Chapter Six offers strategies for using the Object Knowledge Framework in a project development process and includes exercises and brainstorm suggestions for teams working with object-based experiences. Chapters Seven, Eight and Nine include activities and examples involving the concepts transforming objects through design, content and participation.

If a goal for museums is to offer powerful connections between visitors and objects, then thinking about how those interactions happen can be informative in building greater value for those who visit. Similarly, the growing trend toward more explicit care of collections, and the rise of meaning making as an essential component of museum experiences reinforce our need to know the meaning of those object encounters. It may seem obvious that the individual visitor's experience is key to successful exhibitions and programs in museums. Yet, more often than not, the truly unique elements of an individual experience are dismissed as idiosyncratic outliers. Certainly, looking for those commonly shared group experiences with objects is one method that supports good decision making about object use, and this book does not suggest that sound visitor research should be based only on individual experiences. Instead, our purpose is to place the spotlight on the *experiences* that individual people can have with objects as a way of seeing that these encounters do follow patterns that are just as useful for successful and fulfilling planning in museums.

SECTION 1

Thinking About Objects

In this section we explore what it means to think about and know objects in museum settings. We focus on the way that museums can better understand human-object encounters and harness these moments to build better museum experiences. In Chapter One we introduce the ideas of lived experience and how experiences of "knowing" objects in different ways can play an important role in the overall museum process. We present a first look at the Object Knowledge Framework and explain its role and how it suggests new directions for museum practice. As we explore the Framework our goal is to look closely at the connections between three different dimensions of object knowledge. Chapter Two provides an in-depth look at the features of the Object Knowledge Framework and begins to explore the opportunities museums have in making connections with museum visitors. The chapter presents an array of concepts about objects in the world generally, and more specifically within museum settings.

CHAPTER ONE

Object Knowledge

The relationships that people have with objects are as varied as objects themselves. Equally different are the ways that people come to *know* those objects. In part, these diverse ways of knowing stem from an individual's motivation and interests. For example, those who wish to preserve objects for a future generation might focus on the role of an object as something intended for posterity, like donating artworks in support of a new wing for an art museum. Some objects, such as the first dollar bill a restaurant earned, show future viewers evidence of events that occurred in the past. Communities might use objects as examples of shared experiences or traditions, like the butter sculptures found at many state fairs. A museum visitor may know an object as something that provides entertainment, furthers their education, or serves as a touchstone for their life experiences. Each of these instances highlights the informational aspects of the object in relation to different groups. However, they also indicate other ways of knowing objects than just "facts": knowing happens through a person's senses, memory, emotions, and most of all, identity. These alternative ways of knowing objects—the personally and emotionally connected relationships with objects—provide the greatest insight into a new realm for museum work.

As museums continue to define and refine their purposes and roles in communities, and strive to make stronger connections for visitors in their learning and meaning making, it is vital that they pay close attention to their visitors' personal connections to objects. Doing so means that museums will grapple with the idea that the content and meaning of their collections are different for every visitor who comes to see them. In part, these revisions reflect the transition from older, hierarchical models where the collections were typically more important than visitors. Conn (1998) suggested that

Elizabeth Wood and Kiersten F. Latham, "Object Knowledge" in *The Objects of Experience: Transforming Visitor-Object Encounters in Museums*, pp 24-39.

the museum field must make a shift away from a nineteenth century sense of "object-based epistemology," which emphasized the facts and explanation of an object and gave order to the meaning of objects primarily through their visual arrangement. Instead, the idea of an "object-based dialogue" underscores the importance of a shared process: "the object, the presentation, the visitor, even the friends and family accompanying the visitor, jointly participate in an act of meaning" (Wertsch, 2002, p. 115).

Creating opportunities for visitor meaning making is now the preeminent task of most museum and other informal learning methods (Falk & Dierking, 2000; Gurian, 2006; Roberts, 1997). Developing experiences for people that build on their prior knowledge of the world and lead them toward new ideas and conceptions is at the root of contemporary theories of transformative learning (Mezirow, 2000). While meaning making strategies have most recently been at the core of visitor-centered experiences in particular, the study of the role that objects play in this process, particularly in museums and informal learning environments, has had limited exposure.

In some contemporary museums, the idea of *experience* now drives museum planning and management. Finding the right strategies to satisfy a visitor's experience—from amenities such as cafes and gift shops to the topics and content of exhibitions and programs—can dominate the activities of nearly all types of museum workers. In this context, there are some notable museum teams who reconstructed the role of objects within their museum. These renovations are excellent examples of institution-wide philosophical changes that can affect the visitor experience of museum objects dramatically. They are more than a face-lift: they are a large-scale redesign of the role and purpose of museum experiences and activities and are changes to the whole network of the museum. For example in 2006, the Oakland Museum of Art in California (OMCA) undertook a major transformation of philosophy, practice, and process that led to new ways of thinking about creating museum experiences with both visitor and object at the center. This process led the museum's staff through countless discussions, prototypes, evaluation and listening sessions, and conversations about what visitors wanted and needed from their experience at the museum. When reflecting on the process for selecting objects, René de Guzman (2010), senior curator of art, wrote:

> I found it surprising that so much drama surrounded inanimate objects. The curators defended the integrity of pure experience of the object, the educators fought for the object's ability to communicate to a general public, and the conservators and registrars wanted to protect the object from physical dangers and harm. (p. 89)

The Strong Museum in Rochester, New York, underwent a major rebranding and mission revision between 2004 and 2006 to focus on the core components of its collection of toys in order to build a more viable visitor experience through the idea of play. The staff worked to find ways to make meaningful connections between visitors and the museum's objects. By recalibrating its focus from a museum about dolls and toys (just objects) to one about play (people *and* objects) the museum became more evocative for its targeted family audience. Both the OMCA example and the Strong Museum example demonstrate how focusing on an inclusive museum experience for visitors—one which emphasizes objects and visitor interests, ideas, and interpretations—can result in a meaningful change for visitors, museum staff, and overall perception of public value.

Our goal throughout this book is to provide readers with discussion and examples of how objects play a role in visitor meaning making in museum settings. In particular we focus on the balance between museum visitor personal experience, the knowledge and experience of museum staff, and the unique opportunities museums have in creating meaningful encounters with objects. To do this we first investigate the idea of "lived experience" and explore the different ways that visitors come to know and make sense of objects not only in their everyday lives, but also in museum settings.

Lived Experience and the Museum

Ellen Rosenthal, executive director of Conner Prairie Living History Park in Fishers, Indiana, describes the park's goals as "treat[ing] history not as something completed, but as something *lived*, something that grows out of people's experiences and understanding" (Rothstein, 2011, p. C2, emphasis added). This *lived* experience is difficult to describe, and even harder to anticipate, but it is the root of a new way of thinking about the visitor-object encounter in museums. The human urge to seek and make meaning of objects is not generally obvious in everyday activity, and people don't often think about these meanings until they are brought to their attention or revealed to them in some specific way. This is one benefit of using objects in the museum experience: when a visitor's encounter with a museum object raises an awareness in them, they may intentionally seek out a deeper meaning of that object through investigation or inquiry. Certainly, not every object in a museum will trigger this connection, but when it does, that's when the "museum magic" starts to happen (Silverman, 2002).

The lived experience of visitors in the museum, and in particular their lived experiences with objects, is the starting point for the Object Knowledge Framework. Building this perspective for working with the lived experience with objects takes into account the different ways to *know* an object. In particular, the goal is to better understand the human connection and attachment to objects. The Object Knowledge Framework unites the best of contemporary museum practices, and what a museum staff knows about the objects in their collections, with an appreciation for the interests, prior knowledge, and potential personal experiences of the visitors.

The lived experience of something occurs when a person is aware of an experience he or she is having while it is happening. It is, however, not something that a person can make meaning of in the moment they experience it. Instead, people make meaning of a lived experience after the event occurs, often only when they intentionally reflect on it. Imagine hearing your favorite song on the radio: your first reaction might be, "Hey, this is my favorite song, turn it up!" You become aware of what you are hearing and in the moment, take an action (dance, sing, wiggle, smile). Only later, perhaps when prompted, will you be able to explain what hearing that song means to you. The lived experience with an object—knowing the meaning and importance of something—is not just immediate or passing knowledge: it is the kind of knowledge that a person has on deep emotional, physical, and psychological levels. Yet, even this kind of understanding of an object can be hard to process without time for reflection. The more that a person actively connects to and thinks about his or her encounter with an object, the more he or she becomes aware of the experience.

The concepts of lived experience, of intentional focus, and of awareness of those experiences are all part of a philosophy called *phenomenology.* These ideas are threaded throughout this book and form the basis for the Object Knowledge Framework; knowing and using the key principles of phenomenology are especially powerful when applied in the museum setting to stimulate visitor experiences with objects.

Phenomenology is an approach to studying human experience; it does not separate objective and subjective meaning into different categories. Instead, it emphasizes an immediate, sensorial and individual way of seeing the world. Put another way, the outlook of phenomenologists is to use direct experience to understand the many different ways that people come to know the world around them. Most notably though, phenomenologists hold that each person's experience of the world is relative to their own perspective, and it is through this way of knowing that the person is able to make sense of the world around them. Phenomenology is the study of a person's active involvement in the meaning making process, and it helps enhance the overall ways of understanding and knowing the world around us.

Studying the visitor experience of objects phenomenologically can give museum professionals insights into the visitor's *lifeworld*: the immediate, dynamic, and direct world that every person inhabits. The lifeworld is something that each person has, and is always and already there to encounter and be encountered. Imagine a person surrounded by an imaginary bubble: this bubble is the person's lifeworld. The extent of the bubble carries the person's immediate present, their past and their future, and moves with them wherever they go. That bubble becomes part of each environment the person encounters, contributes to it, and is potentially changed by it. As the person goes through the world, he or she see things and knows them in a meaningful way, both in terms of shared knowledge and individual meaning. Each person's bubble is unique—yet, because it is permeable, the meaning the person makes is something that can be accessible to or shared among many different people. In a museum experience, the same principle of the lifeworld applies. Each person's bubble potentially changes when they come into the museum and experience the exhibits. What a person sees comes through all the dimensions of that bubble. An exhibit might elicit a sense of awe and reverence from a wide range of visitors, and that same exhibit may create different levels or types of feelings for individual visitors. At the EMP Museum in Seattle, fans of Jimi Hendrix can revel in seeing actual guitars that he played (and destroyed), while many others might stand and look bemusedly, trying to figure out what the big deal is.

Phenomenology concerns itself with experience, and in particular recognizes that *knowing* the world is *being* in the world, experiencing it. That conception means that people are in effect not separate entities from each other, but rather entwined with the world around them. This is why it can be so hard to truly see how objects influence human experience. Phenomenologists call the idea of this interwoven person-world *intentionality.* It means that as human beings we exist in a world surrounded by objects that are already there, and we cannot avoid them. Given these circumstances we have relationships with those objects. Some relationships with objects are givens because we are familiar with them and have become used to them. Other things in the world are unfamiliar to us, and we become aware of them because of that variation. A chair, for example, is a common object for most people; in the modern world we grow up with chairs and know generally what they are and how to use them. A chair has a certain set of features that make it a chair: a seat, a back, and some way to connect it to the floor, usually its legs. Some chairs are hard, some are squishy, some have arms, but they all have these general characteristics. People don't need to work hard to know they see chairs when entering a room. In a sense, most things with "chair-ness" are background information based on prior experience until something different catches a person's attention.

Now imagine a person walking into a room and seeing something unusual. All the cues in the room suggest that the thing might be a chair, but there's something different about it. The whole thing looks like a tree; the back is very high and has branches at the top. There's an element that looks like a stump, but it might actually be a place to sit. Seeing this difference causes the person to become very aware of that thing that might look like a chair. It draws their attention, and the person needs to consciously or purposefully use their prior experiences to try to make sense of it. They carefully examine a wide range of sensory inputs that helps determine what the thing is. In phenomenology, becoming acutely aware of the experience a person is having is called *consciousness*. Consciousness is a process of making sense of unusual perceptions. For example, a person might experience consciousness of a chair if it is particularly hard, soft, unusual looking, or unfamiliar. Similarly, if a person comes from a culture that does not have chairs, the object moves to the foreground of the experience because of its differences. All of these moments of awareness happen quickly.

Put most simply, consciousness is always the consciousness *of* something. This process of perception involves the body and works through the senses: humans live in and are conscious of the world through their bodies. Bodily knowledge incorporates the traditional five senses, as well as the sensations of time, space, and interpersonal awareness. All of these elements contribute to the way that a person can create meaning or make sense of his or her lived experiences. The meanings of lived experiences are actually quite prevalent in how people describe different events in their lives. A telephone advertisement, for instance, once suggested that through the phone one could "reach out and touch someone"— invoking bodily awareness that might come with talking to a person on the phone. The feeling that "time flies" is another example of a sensory perception through the body. Though it is a constant, people's perception of time varies depending on the activity; that variation of experience is what makes people aware of the passage of time. Recognizing the role of consciousness in the study of visitor-object encounters gives museums ways to think about supporting visitors in their meaning making.

Using these principles of phenomenology, museum staff can better understand the ways that visitors experience exhibits and programs. The visitor encounters an environment of things in the museum, some of which might be background information, while the objects the visitor is less familiar with will advance to the foreground of their awareness. In short, the visitor's lifeworld and their consciousness matter in how they ultimately experience a museum's objects.

A World Consisting of Objects

In the study of phenomenology the idea of objects plays an important role. People are only able to make sense of their existence through things of the world (Heidegger, 1967). As mentioned earlier, this idea of an interconnected person-world reality is called *intentionality*. As people encounter objects, they begin to make sense of the world, and they make meaning from these experiences. An object is like a mirror: as a person gazes on an object, ideas are reflected back at them through the object. These ideas come from their own experiences, through their lifeworld. Imagine, then, what it means when someone encounters an object in a museum setting. Every object has the potential to support a visitor in making meaning, every object has the potential to reflect *something* back onto its viewer, and every object has the potential to create a moment of consciousness within the visitor. Whether the encounter is watching the cables in an exposed elevator shaft, holding an ancient pot, seeing real dinosaur bones, or sitting on a bench looking at art, museums might begin to consider the new thinking on how people experience objects. Objects serve as focal points for bringing ideas, thoughts, and meaning together in the same place: they aid in people's ability to create meaning in the world. That makes every museum object potentially influential and vital in more distinctive ways than has been recognized in the past.

Because humans create meaning in the world through objects, each object can have very different meanings or explanation. Museums use objects as part of a communication process; they are vessels or conduits for explaining or interpreting a message of some kind. The museum visitor is constantly making sense of the object and the museum's interpretation by translating that message into their own experience. This means that both museums *and visitors* are interpreters and translators of objects. Any kind of translation is a complex and careful process that takes into account both the preservation and the embellishment of an original idea—a little bit of art and a little bit of science. Translation of the written word from one language to another can yield any number of versions, and translation of an object in a museum is really no different. With each person who encounters an object the translation may be very precise and informed, or it may be broadly and generally construed.

Beyond recognizing the most obvious physical or material traits of an object, visitors may not have all the tools they need to understand the information contained in the object, and they may want or need more information to help them make sense of what they see in an exhibition or program. Museum interpretation plays this role. As interpreters of objects, museums' goals are to do more than just "translate" objects in exhibitions. This means going beyond restating an object's history, composition, or origin. Instead, it means working to promote visitor experiences that activate stories and emotions about or with the object. Interpretation of objects in museums should be based on a variety of strategies that help visitors make both emotional and intellectual connections. Freeman Tilden's (1957) classic principles of interpretation—provocation instead of information, relating stories to the visitor experience, creating revelation, presentation of the whole—apply now just as much as ever. Yet, it may be that what visitors need is not necessarily more of a museum's interpretation of an object, but a *transformation* of the object into a new way of knowing it. This transformation of the object, whether through innovative display techniques, highlighted content, or opportunities to build on experiences, helps elucidate and draw out the meaning of an object at multiple levels. It can provide potentialities, openings. Museum staff can, in a sense, be "object advocates" and look for the opportunities to use objects in a way that will not only reveal many more layers of information, but will also provide opportunities for visitors to project their own experiences onto objects. All of these strategies allow meaning to be reflected back to the visitor.

Introducing the Object Knowledge Framework

The purpose of the Object Knowledge Framework is to define a process by which people come to know objects in a museum space, and in the world at large. One of the keys to the Object Knowledge Framework is in understanding the relationship between three elements of a museum object encounter:

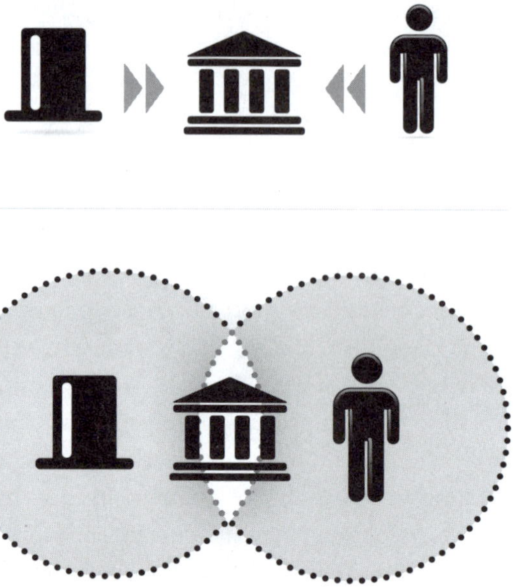

FIGURE 1.1 Visitor-Object Interaction (above). Visitor-Object Encounter (below).

first, what the visitor brings to the experience (their *lifeworld*); second, how the museum positions or transforms the object within that experience (the *objectworld*); and third, what results, if the conditions are right, when the visitor and the object meet in the exhibition or program (the visitor's *unified experience* with the object). This unified experience is very different from an *interaction*, which is the moment wherein a person encounters a thing and does something with it, each of them remaining separate (Figure 1.1 middle). A unified experience is its own thing, a moment that can only exist by the blending of the person's lifeworld and the sensations, perceptions, and awareness they have of the object with the qualities and features of the objectworld (Figure 1.1 bottom).

A visitor takes in the information and meaning of the objectworld through their own lifeworld, which includes various *dimensions* and *reflections* of their own experiences. These dimensions are like different windows on the world; the view from each provides a slightly different angle. Each dimension represents many different ways to know objects. In the same manner, a museum team works to provide a wide range of transformations of the objectworld into a series of experiences and potential meanings.

The Object Knowledge Framework, using these concepts, provides a strategy for guiding museum staff through new approaches to thinking about objects in a museum setting. The more that museum staff reflect on the lived experience that people have with objects, the more the Framework comes to life in the museum experience. In *Plastics Unwrapped* at the University of Washington's Burke Museum in Seattle, visitors confront the widespread use of plastics in everyday life. The exhibit's purpose is to motivate visitors to think about their relationship to plastics in their lives. The exhibit topic draws on the tensions associated with the plastics industry: safety and convenience versus overuse and pollution. Almost immediately the role of the visitor's lifeworld comes into play. *Plastics Unwrapped* certainly elicits familiar feelings for anyone who feels plagued by the sheer numbers of plastic bags they get in a given week, or who worries about the increasing amount of plastic packaging or the inability to recycle it. The exhibit's transformation of plastic objects into compelling visual scenes demonstrates the museum's use of the objectworld to make its point. Visitors see 3,000 plastic bags on the wall—the number of plastic bags given out in the United States, every quarter of a second. Another component demonstrates 1,500 plastic water bottles, lined up in neat rows and columns, as the number that are used every second in the United States. Throughout the exhibit the labels and visual elements suggest alternative ways to think about using plastic, even as they explore the history, science, and cultural role of plastics. In each of these exhibit components the visitor's lifeworld and the objectworld can come together in a unified experience. The strength of the exhibit in creating the potential unified experiences comes in relating the lived experience of some of the more iconic plastic objects—water bottles, plastic bags, and packaging—along with new perspectives on the role of plastics in health and medical advancements. In each instance, what becomes critical in the visitor experience is how they are able to make sense of the issues the museum presents, and then, in what ways they are changed as a result.

The Dimensions of Visitor Lifeworlds

As we explained earlier in the chapter, the lifeworld is like a bubble that surrounds each person. Within that bubble are the person's ways of knowing the world through their past experiences, senses, emotions, and knowledge; we call these *dimensions*. Each person's dimensions are of a different size, shape, and configuration from anyone else's.

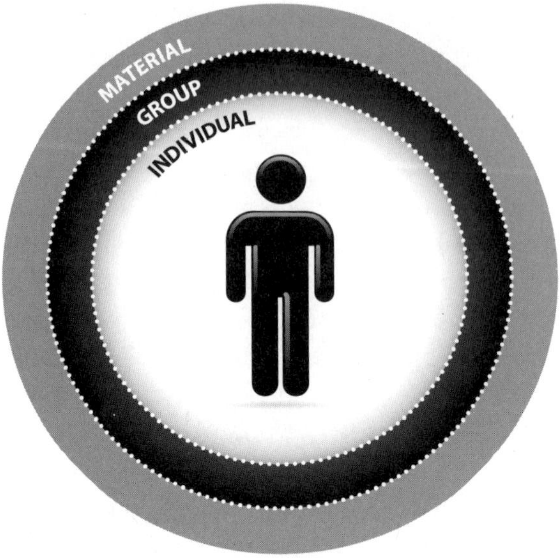

FIGURE 1.2 Dimensions of the Lifeworld.

In the Object Knowledge Framework there are three primary dimensions of the lifeworld: *individual* ways of knowing, *group* ways of knowing, and *material* ways of knowing (Figure 1.2). Each dimension provides the visitor with certain specific pieces of information or perspectives that are relevant at different points in time. Visitors (and museum staff) use aspects of these dimensions of information about an object to make sense of it. How the visitor applies these aspects of their dimensions depends on the many contexts of that particular visit. We separate them out for the purposes of the model, but in the lifeworld, all three are "on" all the time. Ultimately, the three dimensions of object knowledge provide multiple entry points for visitors to better learn from and experience museum objects in meaningful ways.

The *individual dimension* denotes the personal significance of an object to an individual viewer. It is the most immediate, and likely the first, connection a visitor will have to an object. In a visitor-object encounter, the person has a lived experience with the object and comes to some kind of consciousness about the object. They might be thinking about how they *feel* in the space or how they *sense* the object. In addition to providing this immediate sensory knowledge, the individual dimension is also an opening, a threshold, into prior knowledge, experiences, and opinions. This might include the connection a person makes between an object and his or her own identity, a personal narrative or story, or some kind of biographical meaning, association, or connection.

While the individual dimension is something a visitor brings with them, the museum's careful consideration and planning about positioning the object can further support the extent of these personal and emotional transactions. Importantly, the individual dimension influences and informs all the other elements of visitor-object encounter: personal experiences will shape how someone observes the material features of an object, and will inform their group perspectives on its importance. These experiential cues and personal experiences determine to a certain extent how a visitor will direct their attention toward an object in the museum setting.

The *group dimension* draws out a wide assortment of universal experiences and themes, as well as the social, cultural, and historical meanings of objects. This dimension can provide background for meaning, and often illuminates some facet of the object from a shared group perspective. Group dimensions might include things like a person's participation or membership in a particular interest group, a geographic community, broader cultural group, or even their family. This shared nature of the knowledge of an object shapes the group dimension. It is very common for museums to draw from these group interpretations of objects, particularly those that emphasize widely shared histories or cultural activities.

The *material dimension* highlights the physical nature of an object. It includes aspects of the composition, the outward appearance, and other aesthetic elements. It also includes how the museum chooses to present the object's physical presence in the space. Museums frequently use material dimensions to describe or interpret objects. The material dimension and physical elements of an object are not solely restricted to verbal or visual information gathering. The material dimension can (and we believe should) also include aspects of touching or feeling objects to further inform the visitor experience with the object (Wood & Latham, 2011).

Defining the Objectworld

Just as museum visitors arrive with dimensions of their lifeworld, objects bring qualities to the encounter. The objectworld consists of all of the information, actions, events, and people associated with the object over its entire life, plus the way in which the museum has transformed that information into a museum experience. This objectworld reflects the spectrum of human experiences as well as the function or role of that object in human life. The objectworld dimensions include all of the material and physical characteristics of the object, as well as group and individual dimensions (Figure 1.3). In the

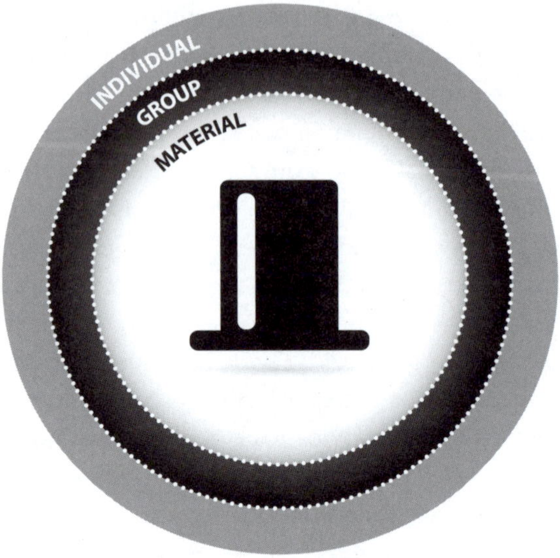

FIGURE 1.3 Dimensions of the Objectworld.

case of the objectworld, the group dimensions include broad human themes and global perspectives, and the individual dimension includes specific stories about the object, its owners, and the local circumstances where it existed. Each object dimension represents different ways that museum staff can think about positioning and transforming objects for the museum experience.

The *material dimensions* of the objectworld consist of the physical composition and construction of the object. The material qualities also include texture, shape, size, weight, color, smell, sound, levels of decay, and so on. Unfortunately, access to many of these sensory qualities is difficult and sometimes off-limits to museum visitors. However, more and more museums are working toward achieving multi-sensory access to objects. There is no doubt that the material dimensions of the objectworld, even with limited access, provide very important opportunities for visitor-object encounters.

The object's *group dimensions*, broad human themes and global perspectives, cut across time, place, and people. These narrative themes help visitors think about broader connections to other people and other issues, and reflect possible human experiences across time and place. These broad themes are often abstract concepts like family and kinship, or ideas of love, beauty, and happiness. They may represent aspects of commerce and trade, shelter, religion, cooking, play, gender, and so forth. A museum may position an object to show global stories of human existence, or the object's function in a range of situations. For example, the positioning of a fountain pen in an exhibit can evoke aspects of human progress, but it can just as easily be a tool for communication, or stand as an example of craftsmanship.

Looking at the object's *individual dimensions,* distinctive personal connections relate to an object, such as a prior owner of the object, the curator's vision, or a group of people who might have used similar objects. Take a guitar for example: the individual connections that the owner has will be different from those that the curator might have or even a group of guitar-playing fans will have, yet each of these connections is a valid way to interpret the guitar's meaning. The stories about the use of the object by that person can evoke particular feelings or memories in a visitor. Information related to the local circumstances or specific situations can shed light on the events and circumstances of a specific time and place. From this vantage point the object might reflect the actions of humans in very particular detail. The meaning of the fountain pen described in the preceding paragraph might reflect universal ideas of human communication when broadly conceived, but when seen from an individual dimension it serves as evidence of the power of a president signing an important piece of legislation such as the United States Civil Rights Act of 1964.

As we have said, as the visitor engages with the objectworld, the dimensions of their lifeworld will inform the extent to which they might have a unified experience with the object. To show how these two worlds come together, let's imagine an exhibit with a hat. This particular hat is a top hat, often called a stovepipe hat. In fact, United States President Abraham Lincoln once wore this hat. Once the information about the hat connects to a particular time, an owner, and when the owner used the hat, the role of the objectworld dimensions is evident. This visually iconic object (material dimensions) has come to symbolize many aspects of American history (group dimensions). The hat evokes the American Civil War, knowledge of presidents, and even of the Lincoln assassination (group dimensions). The individual dimensions of the hat are the stories and background information on Abraham Lincoln, but might also be about the person who made the hat or gave it to Lincoln. Now, applying the dimensions from the visitor's lifeworld, a new view of the hat comes into focus. Has the visitor seen the hat before? Who was with them? Why were they there? Also, many Americans are familiar with this particular hat from history lessons in school (group dimension) or making a hat out of construction paper (material dimension). The visitor may also connect by thinking back to being a child, learning about Lincoln with other students in the classroom, remembering the teacher and even the room in which he or she learned these things, and echoing the thoughts and feelings of their own childhood (individual dimensions). The resonances of the individual experience (a lived experience) complete the meaning of the hat.

How a museum chooses to position and transform these dimensions of the objectworld depends greatly on aspects of design, ways of explaining content, and strategies for visitor participation and contact with objects. How this works in museum practice is the focus of Section Three, *Object Transformations*.

The Unified Experience

As described in the preceding section, when the visitor and object come together, the intermingling of the visitor's lifeworld and the objectworld can form a unified experience. When the combination of the lifeworld and objectworld creates deep meaning or a powerful lived experience, the visitor has a unified experience. These unified experiences are sometimes felt as an "Aha!" experience, a holy experience, a moment of awe or wonder, or an experience of enchantment or delight. The unified experience comes about when an intentional and purposeful transformation of the object creates a moment of consciousness or awareness by the museum visitor. Importantly, the unified experience results from a commingling of the visitor's dimensions and the dimensions of the object. Of course, the dimensions that the visitor brings to the experience are largely unknown to the museum. However, museum staff can begin to gather possible insights into what visitors will bring to the experience through various planning processes and front-end research on visitor expectations, prior knowledge, interests, and understanding of the lived experience of objects (Korn, 2004). Further, the more that staff understand their visitors in terms of age, purpose of the visit, local context, or visitor familiarity with the topic, the better the planning can support successful overall experiences. Each of these aspects of audience research helps in creating conditions to support a unified visitor-object experience.

Forward Thinking

Using the Object Knowledge Framework to transform visitor experiences with objects, museum teams can begin to think differently about how to create those encounters. As a museum visitor notices an object, they may begin to direct their attention toward it, and may begin to sift through their various dimensions as a way to know that object. In the chapters that follow, we provide a deep exploration of the Object Knowledge Framework as the foundation for object-based experience in museums. Thinking about these intersections between visitors and objects, understanding how visitors comprehend objects in museums and related environments, can help museum practitioners recognize the ways that visitors make meaning from these encounters. Building on this kind of object knowledge will bring greater attention to the significance of visitors' own background and knowledge, and will help visitors better relate to objects that previously might not have interested them.

In this chapter we focused on the ways that individual people come to know objects in museum settings. The individual perspective may be the end result of the visitor-object encounter, but it includes contributions from the ideas and thoughts of many scholars. In the next chapter we explore the components of the Object Knowledge Framework in greater detail and look specifically at how different fields of practice study look at human-object encounters.

CHAPTER TWO

The Object Knowledge Framework

One of the unique aspects of museum work is the vast array of scholarship that informs the approaches to developing exhibitions and programs. Accessing scholarship from a variety of fields of study gives museums multiple ways to contemplate objects and multiple ways to think about how those objects matter in a visitor's experience. Each of these disciplines shapes the museum field in some way regarding the purposes of objects, how objects are incorporated into daily life, and how objects function in the human world. In this chapter we explore the Object Knowledge Framework and how these multiple disciplines view objects and object-based interactions. We focus on the components of the Object Knowledge Framework to show how we created it, and explain the influences that drove our process.

Among the most influential fields of study informing the role of objects in museum experiences are anthropology, archaeology, psychology, history, material culture studies, and education. *Anthropology* tends to focus on objects in terms of human culture and society, whereas *archaeology* analyzes the role of objects of human history and pre-history. *Psychology* looks at people's cognitive, social and behavioral connections to objects and can inform museum visitor motivations and preferences. *History* and *material culture* investigate the relationship between people and objects in terms of social organization, functions, and attitudes. *Education* positions objects as tools and strategies for learning experiences. Adopting an interdisciplinary approach is useful in thinking creatively and more expansively about visitor encounters with objects. The different fields' approaches presented here illuminate the possibilities for new kinds of visitor experiences in museums.

As described in Chapter One, the Object Knowledge Framework relies on the *lived experience* of objects and the vastly different ways that people

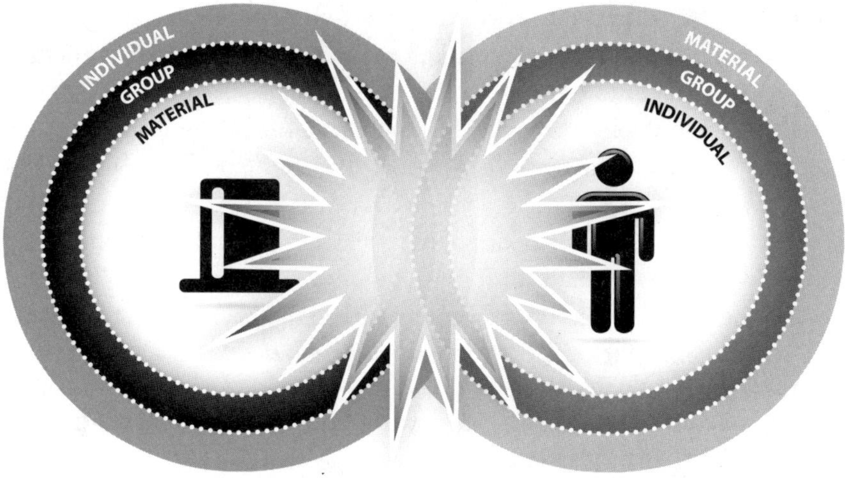

FIGURE 2.1 The Object Knowledge Framework.

and objects meet. These intersections of visitor and object, especially those intentionally positioned within the museum setting, can promote rich experiences for museum visitors. While phenomenology and lived experience are the philosophical ground for thinking about the visitor experience with objects, many different disciplinary traditions and perspectives also support this orientation to museum practice. No single field or discipline necessarily looks at the whole context of the object; rather, each favors a particular role or purpose for the use and inclusion of objects in human experience. We have mixed and re-mixed ideas from multiple sources to arrive at a well-rounded concept of objects in the museum experience. The Object Knowledge Framework is an attempt to blend these ideas together into a useful tool for thinking about objects as part of a museum visitor's experience (Figure 2.1). In the previous chapter we outlined the primary elements of the Object Knowledge Framework as components of the objectworld, the dimensions of the visitor lifeworld, and unified experiences with an object. In the following section we examine each of these in detail.

Components of the Objectworld

We call the museum's positioning or transformation of an object within a visitor experience the *objectworld.* This positioning is not the same as using the results of an object analysis to present information; instead the focus is on creating the conditions for a relationship between an *object* in the museum setting and the visitor experience. The objectworld consists of all the information that a museum can share about the material, group, and individual dimensions of an object.

There are multiple entry points for understanding the idea of an object and how museum visitors come to "know" objects. The word *object*, in the sense of a tangible item, is derived from a Latin verb phrase, meaning to put something in the way of a person so they will see it (Ayto, 1990) or as something sought after or aimed at (Oxford English Dictionary, 1989). Similarly, philosophers define objects as things toward which people direct attention and action, which includes both tangible and intangible objects (Harman, 2011; Heidegger, 1967). Tangible objects are the physical objects present in the world and ready for human use. Intangible objects come in the form of ideas, thoughts, actions, and reflections. Keeping with these definitions, objects in the museum are all the *things* toward which the visitor will direct their attention and actions. Museums put objects on display in hopes that visitors will direct their attention to them. Museums might use tangible objects to represent certain intangible exhibition and programmatic concepts or ideas.

Another aspect of the objectworld is based on visitor access to an object that supports their ability to gather information about it. Human ways of knowing are wide-ranging and can include aspects of sensory perception, language, reasoning and logic, emotions, intuitions, imagination, faith, and so on. Thinking about different ways of knowing in the museum context is critical in designing successful exhibitions and programs. Not only are the strategies that give visitors access to different ways of knowing important, but so too is the source of that knowledge. Lisa Roberts (1997) suggests that "the once prevalent view that knowledge is objective and verifiable has been widely challenged by the notion that knowledge is socially constructed and shaped by individuals' particular interests and values" (p. 2). Similarly, practices in museums are moving away from hierarchical classification systems and disciplinary-specific agreements on the nature of certain ideas. Instead, they are becoming more and more focused on the multi-layered connections between objects and ideas, why objects and ideas came to be, and perhaps most importantly, how they are all interrelated (Hooper-Greenhill, 1992). Just as a curator has deep content knowledge of a particular subject matter, visitors can come with an equally deep, but different perspective on the same subject.

This diversity of ideas and knowledge is to be expected in contemporary museum practice: "Whether we agree or disagree with one another in how we experience the world, we must appreciate why and how such agreements are reached" (Hein, 2000, p. xiii). Accepting the multiple ways of knowing in the museum involves paying greater attention to the needs and interest of the museum visitor, as well as the role that museum staff play in selecting, creating, curating, and developing the museum experience.

Throughout the last several decades of museum scholarship, several authors have used the term *object knowledge* to refer to the kind of information that visitors might gain from or use in looking at objects. Most notably, Thomas Schlereth's (1992) definition of object knowledge was focused on museum literacy, or the ways that museums teach visitors to "read" objects. As a historian and scholar of material culture, Schlereth adopted an orientation to object knowledge that emphasizes how visitors view objects from both analytical and interpretive perspectives. However, his view limits the individual knowledge that visitors might draw from (or bring to) the objects. Instead of visitors interpreting objects from personal experience, knowledge, and meaning, Schlereth's focus is on the visitor's interpretation of social history and culture. Other scholarly conceptions of object knowledge range from identification and description of an object's properties to inform a museum's exhibition or collection (Fleming, 1974; Prown, 1982), to more recent examinations of the deeply personalized or embodied experiences of objects (Duensing, 2002; Wehner & Sear, 2010).

The Role of Context

Objects, whatever they may be, are essential elements of any visitor experience. The wide-ranging strategies that museum exhibitions and programs employ to stimulate visitor interactions with objects are part of what composes the objectworld. Design, spatial configurations, and other sensory clues influence the ways that visitors make meaning. The visitor mixes this information of the objectworld with his or her own lifeworld to make meaning. A visitor's object knowledge, then, is a blend of information of the objectworld with the information from his or her own lifeworld. In the museum setting different contextual elements create this blended experience.

Some of the more interesting arguments made around the idea of context and knowing objects arise from explorations into the importance of multiple meanings or simultaneous interpretation of ideas. Many of these positions emerged during the later part of the twentieth century in fields like archaeology. Ian Hodder's (1986) suggestion that "each object exists in many relevant dimensions at once" (p. 139) reiterates the notion that different observers can make multiple and equally valid interpretations of an object at the same time. Hodder proposed four aspects that could define an object's context: time, space or location, use or purpose, and cultural classification. To illustrate his point, Hodder explains these strategies in identifying pots. When investigating the design and purpose of pottery, the archaeologist uses contextual information in total rather than looking at distinctive elements of pot design or markings. In this manner the information about the time period may also suggest the object's purpose. The space or location of the object might also inform its purpose or cultural classification, and so on. What is most critical about this orientation is that it is not simply the features of the object itself that provide meaning; rather, it is its whole context that provides clues and information. This is an important orientation for the idea of the Object Knowledge Framework and vital for considering it in the museum setting.

Hodder's notion of context is equally important for how the museum visitor might make sense of an object's meaning. Knowing something about the time, space, purpose, and cultural significance of objects adds to a visitor's ability to know more about it. However, this is not the only aspect of how visitors make meaning of the objects they see. As we discussed in Chapter One, in addition to the information and interpretations provided by the curator or exhibit team, the visitor comes with their own process for examining and thinking about objects based on their life experiences and perspectives. Visitor interpretation of an object changes rapidly based on information from various dimensions of their lifeworld and that of the objectworld. The idea that an object can have multiple meanings, and that those meanings are not fixed, shapes a visitor's ability to make sense of what they are looking at.

Recognizing that objects can mean different things to different people in different places and at different times provides a strong rationale for anticipating these variations in object meanings in a museum exhibition. Imagine, for example, the importance of a farmer discovering an old-looking object his field: what to him is a novel curio might in fact be one of the famed Emperor Qin's Terracotta Warriors. The importance of a find like this might seem obvious to us now, but we can surely imagine the countless priceless objects that were carted away in trashcans or destroyed because at the time they appeared to be worthless to someone else.

As an object moves from its natural setting into a museum it takes on another level of meaning. It now stands in for a particular person, time, place, event, or situation; in other words, it is a representation of something. This change in its reality is called *museality* (Maroevic, 1991). When an object is musealized, it goes through a process of physical or conceptual extraction from its original, natural, or cultural environment, giving it museal status and transforming it into a museum object (International Committee on Museology, 2009). When a museum presents the object in an exhibition, one reality (the thing) represents another reality (the event, person, or idea). Knowing this complicated nature of museality and the multiple meanings that any context provides to an object is one more reason for museum staff to look more holistically at objects, especially when those objects are in a museum setting.

Closely related to the notion of museality is the concept of a *document*, which comes from Document Studies (a related field of Library and Information Science). Like the musealized object, a document is a concrete or symbolic thing that is intentionally preserved for the purpose of representing or proving an idea (Briet, 2006). Imagine, for instance, a tiger in a museum. It is not a real, living, breathing tiger—instead it is a document to show us what a tiger is. It is no longer a "tiger," but rather a "tiger in a museum" (Hudson, 1977). Documentalists use the term "document" to denote any physical information resource or any expression (a representation) of human thought rather than limiting it to specific text-bearing media (Buckland, 1991, 1998). This concept is wholly inclusive and allows the definition of documents to include an array of objects. The meanings of documents and museal objects, once they enter the museum, are layered on top of their preexisting meanings. In this example, the tiger, once a living thing, becomes part of a museum diorama. Now it represents both live tigers as well as tigers in museum dioramas. Niels Lund, a Norwegian documentalist, describes this kind of complementarity of documents as existing fully as 100% mental concept, 100% social concept, and 100% material concept (Lund, 2004). In short, a document, or an object, is never just a bit of this and a bit of that; it is 100% of every meaning one can ever imagine.

A wonderful example of the museum object as a document is not a tiger, but a taxidermied lion called "Simba," featured in the Milwaukee Public Museum's Masai Lion Hunt diorama in the African galleries (Figure 2.2). The diorama depicts several Masai hunters fighting a ferocious, snarling lion. Yet the true backstory of this lion is completely different than what is on display. During one of the museum's many research expeditions in the 1920s the team bought a lion cub from group of Masai who found it after a grass fire. The team members named him Simba and, after the expedition

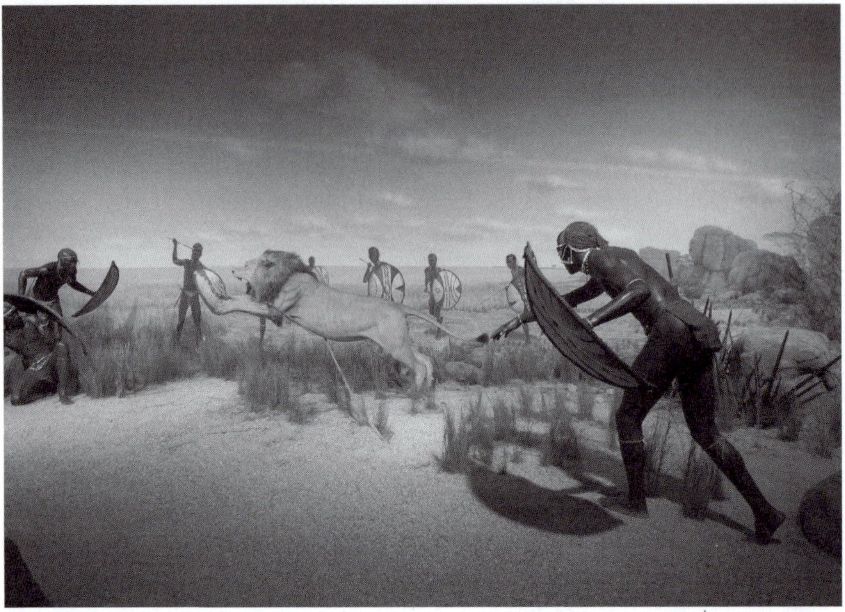

FIGURE 2.2 Simba at The Milwaukee Public Museum. Photo by Elee Wood.

ended, brought him back to the museum. After he had lived for a while on the museum's roof, Simba museum staff transferred him to the Milwaukee zoo for better care. He died of old age and was brought back to the museum to be preserved. "No other museum would have placed him in an African diorama as an example of a wild lion, but Sim was a part of this museum" (Milwaukee Public Museum, 2007, p. 15). Educators now regularly share this story as part of museum programs. As school visitors encounter Simba in the African gallery, they learn the whole story of how he came to be in the museum. Knowing Simba's story builds on the visitor knowledge, not only about the lion, but about how the museum created its dioramas and what they would not necessarily see just from looking: the lion is not just a lion in an exhibit.

Semiotics and the Role of Meaning

Another aspect of explaining meaning making and ways of knowing objects comes from the field of semiotics. While there are many branches and subfields of semiotics that influence the study of material culture, we draw our semiotic foundations from pragmatic approaches where the mediation between objects and meaning plays a significant role (Peirce, 1934). A very basic view of Peirce's semiotics is of a three-way relationship between a representation of something or someone, the subject matter of the representation, and various translations or interpretations of those ideas. Peirce suggested that meaning develops through the connections between these three elements. There is a vast range of representations that a person might make, and these meanings are based on the expanding possibilities that ebb and flow throughout an experience. For museums this means that the kinds of meaning that a visitor might attach to an object might vary considerably depending on how they see an object, what they focus on, and what knowledge they bring to the encounter. While Peirce's ideas are very complex, what is important is the active interplay between meaning, person, and object.

One application of Peirce's ideas focuses on the importance of a person's encounter with the object. Taborsky (1990) argues that meaning is not inherent in objects, but is socially assigned. Knowledge about an object does not necessarily exist prior to a person's contact with the object or through an impartial or uninfluenced view; rather, a person's knowledge about an object comes through actively using it or engaging in some form of dialogue with it. This action occurs through a dynamic process wherein object and observer come together to shape and form meaning. In the moment that object and observer come together, meaning is established. Eileen Hooper-Greenhill (2000) provides a similar explanation of a "seer" and the "seen." The "seer" directs her gaze through a particular place or stance, and what she "sees" can vary depending on how the "seer" understands the object. Meaning exists in the intersection of objects in an exhibition space and the people who come to that space. Therefore, the ultimate interpretive lens is the union of the visitor who brings his or her experience *and* the translation by the museum staff of the object in the museum context.

In a museum experience, a visitor's responses to objects come from broader cultural knowledge, prior knowledge and personal experiences in addition to informational aspects provided by museum staff. This array of responses can give a wide range of unanticipated meanings to an exhibition, but it also means that exhibition or program settings contribute to visitors' meaning making. Through the environment, museum objects can become familiar, or create feelings of belonging through unspoken, or tacit, responses and sometimes through physical reactions. The museum serves as a translator, interpreter, and transformer of ideas, relationships, and points of view through its exhibitions and in particular how objects are used to shape experiences. The important lesson in this work is how the presentation of an object contributes to a visitor's potential unified experience.

Looking Closely at the Visitor's Lifeworld

As we described in Chapter One, visitors bring their own interests and knowledge to the museum experience. The Object Knowledge Framework incorporates three dimensions of experience and knowledge—individual, group, and material—that constitute the visitor's lifeworld. We use these dimensions as a structure to encourage a broader way of conceptualizing visitor-object encounters. At any given time within the lifeworld, one dimension may be more prominent or more active than the others, but each one contributes in some way to a unified visitor-object experience. Using these orientations to inform practice demonstrates the importance of the visitor's worldview and of how museum staff situates the object within an exhibition.

Personal Connections

The role of personal or individual experience of objects is one of the most significant aspects in changing traditional museum-based thinking about objects. The individual dimension of the Framework involves the complex and intricate array of meanings that a person can make with and through object encounters. Personal connections to objects are similarly vast and varied, but this does not mean that intentionally thinking about individual connection to objects is out of reach for museums. Perhaps the most useful conception of the individual dimension is Falk and Dierking's (1992, 2000) contextual model of experience. The contextual model illuminates all the ways that a visitor takes in and experiences the museum as a whole. The elements of personal, sociocultural, and physical contexts clearly echo the dimensions of the lifeworld. However, these three contexts are much more reliant on the nature of the overall experience seen broadly through the eyes of the individual than on direct connection or encounter with museum objects. Even so, the contextual model is useful as a starting point to consider the potential relationship that a visitor can have with objects throughout the museum experience.

The individual dimension of the lifeworld focuses on the way that personal relationships with objects can provide meaning for visitors. The work of Louise Rosenblatt (1978) provides an interesting perspective on individual reactions to literary texts that inform visitor-object encounters in museums. Rosenblatt articulates a continuum of reading between "efferent" encounters, those filled mostly with technical bits of information gathering, and those that are more "aesthetic," the kind of in-the-moment reading where the reader is deeply focused on living through and with the text. According to Rosenblatt, while most reading moves back and forth between the two ends of the continuum, it is in the aesthetic moments of reading where the work becomes more like a "poem," not in the literary sense, but in a way that deeply connects the reader to the signs and symbols presented in the text. Further, the reader derives the poem from the feelings, senses, attitudes, and emotions that come from the transaction with the text. The active process of connecting to and engaging with the words, meanings, and associations contribute to making the reading "an experience," and one that promotes the reader's consciousness of the relationship between the text and herself. The concept of reader, text, and poem become powerful analogies to the museum experience when we translate these into the Object Knowledge Framework. In particular, the reader represents the museum visitor; the text is the object (or exhibition); and the poem represents a unified visitor experience with an object (Latham, 2007).

Cognitive and developmental psychology often examine the role of human-object relationships and the ways in which encounters with objects shape both cognition and identity-development. Cognitive psychologists look at human-object relationships and how humans know objects in the world. This perspective includes how we as humans recognize objects as permanent entities, as things with properties, or as things that humans handle and manipulate (Hood & Santos, 2009). Important work conducted by developmental psychologists in the 1970s and 1980s around identity helps illuminate important relationships between people and their objects. Csikszentmihalyi and Rochberg-Halton (1981) described the meaning of objects as a structure of selfhood that provides opportunities for action, contemplation, and creativity. They suggested that material objects "constitute the framework of experience that gives order to our otherwise shapeless selves" (p. 16). Objects promote a wide range of actions and thoughts through expanding or restricting the scope of a person's worldview. They hold significance in our understanding of the world, notably through an interpretation of the past. In using the Object Knowledge Framework, the museum's careful selection and intentional inclusion of the object that acknowledges a visitor's sense of self can expand the potential to stimulate personal meaning.

Sherry Turkle, well known for her research on the psychology of humans and technology, presents the idea of *evocative* objects—things that serve as "companions to our emotional lives or as provocations to thought" (2007, p. 5). Drawing heavily from the psychoanalytic traditions of Freud and Winnicot, as well as child psychologist Jean Piaget and anthropologist Claude Levi-Strauss, Turkle's work emphasizes the importance of objects in everyday settings and the extent to which these object connections reveal both interpersonal relationships and broad emotional connections. Turkle's work on evocative objects draws together a variety of narrative essays written about objects as wide ranging as a cello, a car, apples, and a vacuum cleaner. She pairs each author's reflections with a theorist's interpretation to inform the ways of knowing objects as active constituents of human life, or "life companions," as Turkle puts it (p. 9). Among these essays, David Mitten's contribution, "The Axe Head," mingles the history of the 5,000-year-old axe head and its material features with the lives of his father and grandfather. The object serves as a connection to his own timeline, as well as the history of a people long past. As Mitten writes, "I owe it a great deal, for it serves as a special talisman, perhaps even a guide, that led me to my lifelong path as a teacher and archaeologist" (2007, p. 125).

Objects like the axe head represent the kind of things people grow accustomed to, connect with, and use to access memories, feelings, and emotions. Seeing this depth of emotion in the museum setting is somewhat uncommon; very deep personal connections to an object are typically based on that of the original owners or users of that object, not on the visitor.

Anthropologist Jenny Hoskins (1998) describes a different kind of personal relationship with objects that involves *biographical,* or person-centered, objects that are localized, particular, and individualized, and *cosmos-centered* objects that are globalized, generalized, and mechanically reproduced. Biographical objects bring another layer of meaning for a person's identity and self-hood through time, space, and self. They grow old, worn and tattered along with a person. The object is limited to the same space as the owner, becoming rooted in the same world; the object "serves as witness" to the everyday activities of the owner. In comparison, the cosmos-centered object is always fresh and new, it exists everywhere and nowhere in particular, and is de-centered from shaping the identity of the person. The Object Knowledge Framework draws on the biographical elements of an object within the museum setting, but recognizes that they are not just about the story of a particular object's owner. These biographical elements are something that could be part of a visitor's own narrative, or some form of story they connect with, or might serve as a witness to a particular event.

Museum exhibitions rarely suggest many personal connections to objects. Most often, these connections are simply references to the original owner, maker, or user of the object. However, to begin to truly use the Object Knowledge Framework, museum staff should shift their thinking to recognize that each visitor will make her own connection to an object. As with Turkle's evocative objects, Hoskins's biographical objects, and Rosenblatt's idea of reader response theory, the objects in the museum experience can further connect visitors with a wide range of emotions, feelings, and relationships. Examples of these relationships are the focus of Section Two, *Object Relationships*.

Shared and Collective Knowledge

Perhaps the most common scholarly orientation and practical display of objects in the museum reflects the group knowledge of the object. Group knowledge consists of all of the various ways that people have collective knowledge of the world. This might be through a close connection such as membership within a family or, more broadly, through association with an interest group. Group knowledge might also include shared stories representing broader cultural values. For example, the Mill City Museum in Minneapolis showcases different types of flour and cooking utensils used by family groups from Poland, Somalia, and Laos. The family stories about flour help to demonstrate the varieties of group knowledge within the Framework. Whereas the individual dimension of the Framework underlines aspects of identity and sense of self, the group dimension emphasizes collective knowledge and the information that groups of people commonly share.

Within the Object Knowledge Framework, a portion of a person's knowledge of an object stems from their general awareness of it, commonly shared stories, collective history, and so on. In many cases an object gains some kind of legitimacy or sense of value and meaning through various cultural or communal practices. These can be as simple as the shared functional meaning of everyday objects like a chair or a desk or more complex as in the shared meaning across more distinctive groups such as a communion chalice or a campaign button. For much of the history of museums, the idea of shared or group knowledge has been based largely on curatorial knowledge, research, and interpretation of objects.

A great deal of object information stems from disciplinary traditions in anthropology, archaeology, history, natural history, science, and art history.

All of these traditions work from various forms of a shared knowledge base on subject content. The level of expertise that museums provide around their objects is part of what makes museums powerful learning institutions. In certain situations though, museums may not explicitly define the shared knowledge base for the visitor; instead, the exhibition or program might present assumed or accepted knowledge as the way to understand the object. Often the visitor's experience will overlap with this shared knowledge in some way, and in other cases the group knowledge the visitor brings can be in conflict with what they see in an exhibition.

In addition to curatorial expertise, drawing on a wider background of information and collective knowledge that the visitor might bring becomes an important strategy for exhibition development. For example, in a typical dinosaur exhibition at a natural history museum, most visitors know or can understand that the enormous set of bones belongs to something called "dinosaur" and not "mouse." The exhibit might provide all the necessary information on the taxonomy of the species and its place in the long tale of natural history. However, while the taxonomic orientation to the exhibit might be grounded in good scientific display practices, the same visitor may not know how to identify particular bones, recognize the difference between a fossil and a cast of a fossil, or know the significance of a complete skeleton. In fact, the visitor may have gleaned their group dimension on this thing called "dinosaur" from popular sources, like movies, books, or children's toys. Museum staff become information brokers and object advocates by developing strategies for displaying objects that help the visitor make sense of what they already know and what they see in an exhibit. Recognizing the differences between group understandings provides opportunities to link expert knowledge to popular knowledge.

The group narratives and stories that visitors bring to a museum experience may not have the same rigor as curatorial preparation, but their knowledge and ways of knowing the objects are just as valid (Roberts, 1997). These communal ideas and orientations to museum objects can become starting points for forms of discovery and exploration, and can propose new orientations for thinking about, encountering, and *experiencing things.* In the dinosaur exhibition described in the preceding paragraph, the exhibit might include different lenses of knowledge such as historic or artistic views of dinosaurs, or descriptions and explanation of dinosaurs from various cultural groups outside of the museum's mainstream audience, or even provide the conflicting views that are ever present in scientific study.

The shared, group dimensions of the Object Knowledge Framework are unquestionably an important feature of a museum visitor's experience. The kinds of knowledge that museums work with to explain and interpret objects often rely on common and collective understanding of topics and ideas. Additionally, the Framework suggests that the group dimension is not the only information a visitor will use when encountering an object and is not always the first dimension that they use. More importantly, knowing the evolution of the underlying and implicit nature of museum practices can help museum staff re-focus the possibilities that future museum experiences provide.

Materiality

The material dimension includes visitor encounters with the physical nature of objects and the sensory experience of those objects. The most obvious element of an object, at least in the museum setting, is its physical presence. The material makeup of an object is simply what it is made of: its shape, form, weight, and construction. The sensory experience of an object, another aspect of its material dimension, comes from the classic five human senses: sight, smell, taste, touch, and hearing. Sensory experiences may also include other forms of perception such as time, movement, temperature, etc. Together the ideas of the physical and sensory components of objects form the concept of *materiality*.

The idea of materiality acknowledges knowing through an embodied engagement with physical things. It draws on the various characteristics of an object that human beings experience through their senses (Dudley, 2010). Objects become important sites for perceptions, emotions, and senses (Knappert, 2005). Recent work, such as that of Dudley (2010), makes the case that "through our sensory experience of them, objects have some potential for value and significance in their own right, whether or not we are privy to any information concerning their purpose or past" (p. 2). While the Object Knowledge Framework incorporates ideas of materiality and sensory experiences like this, we believe that museum experiences should incorporate an expansive view of these intersections that allows visitors to unify thinking, doing, and feeling through transactions with objects. In the museum, objects invite interaction, and thus have the potential to bring about deeply felt memories, ideas, and emotions. Ensuring that all people have access to these aspects of objects is essential to building visitor-object encounters.

Learning from objects in the museum setting often begins with the material nature of the object. Many physical qualities of an object and the extent to which the museum employs those features provide information and context for the museum visitor. The benefits of having real, tangible things within the museum environment are part of what makes it unique. In particular, several material qualities of objects provide visitors with multiple avenues for learning conversations. Leinhardt and Crowley (2002) identified four features of objects that lend credibility to the value of visitor-object encounters. First is the resolution and density of the sensory information about an object. This might include textures, smells, sounds, colors, or weight. The elements of resolution and density of sensory information yield valuable perceptions for visitors. Likewise, the scale of an object—whether very large or very small—provides the opportunity for visitors to gain perspective on the relationship between themselves and an object. A third feature is the authenticity of an object that incorporates the historical and cultural connections and meaning. Finally, the value or uniqueness of an object also contributes to visitor perceptions of an object. Whether the object is *the* spacesuit worn by Neil Armstrong as he walked on the moon, or *the* Declaration of Independence, it shares an important connection to history. Similarly the value of these objects depends on their limited availability and limited access.

In each of these examples, the material dimension is difficult to separate from the group and individual dimensions, showing the importance of the integration of these ideas. Certainly in the case of the four features just described, a visitor's understanding of the authenticity or value of an object stems not only from its material value but also from its group value. Not surprisingly, the three dimensions of the lifeworld often overlap with the dimensions of the objectworld. We use these dimensions in Object Knowledge Framework to illuminate the many ways that visitors come to know and make meaning of objects in a museum setting. By breaking down the components of visitor experiences into more discrete pieces, museum practitioners can begin to rethink ways of integrating this knowledge into exhibitions and programs.

Defining Experiences

When the visitor's lifeworld merges with the objectworld in a meaningful way, the visitor might have a *unified experience.* In this moment the object and the visitor exist in the same space and the visitor creates new knowledge about themselves and the object. The interactions and experiences that people have generate the capacity to be transformational because of this unified experience.

Philosopher and education reformer John Dewey wrote: "life goes on in an environment; not merely *in* it but because of it, through interaction with it" (1934, p. 13). Throughout our lives, we encounter a wide range of experiences—some leading toward growth and fulfillment, others less so. Dewey has had a major influence on museums, and his ideas about the role of objects within lived experience are a major source of inspiration for thinking about the many ways that people make meaning from their encounters with objects.

Three of Dewey's ideas, *experience, unity, and transaction,* are pivotal to the Object Knowledge Framework. First, an *experience* is the most profound moment a person can have. It emerges from a focused, purposeful interaction with one's surroundings, including other humans. The pattern of experience is never-ending; it often begins with something catching our attention or through *disequilibrium* and is always moving toward resolution. People experience disequilibrium through some kind of tension or problem that often creates confusion, doubt, or uncertainty. They seek to resolve that doubt through satisfaction or knowledge that creates a new view on the world. Artworks are often good examples of the experience of disequilibrium. A visitor may view a particular work of art with a growing sense of confusion. As the viewer wrestles with the image, she may take time to look more closely, read a label, or discuss the image with others to find some form of resolution about what she sees. In this experience, her attention has been captured by her perceived disequilibrium of the painting, which then leads her to work on resolving this piqued awareness, which then leads to discussion with others or more individualized investigation.

The ultimate action is to balance and reconcile the tension that comes from the experience—this is Dewey's idea of *unity.* This balance develops through a person's perception of the events, objects, and interactions that stimulate wonder and interest. We include the ideas of unity and experience in our concept of a unified visitor experience with an object. The visitor's effort to make sense of the object through the dimensions of the lifeworld is part of how they seek to balance the tensions of an experience. In the museum setting these experiences can vary depending on the person: they might, for example, be the experience of seeing a favorite work of art in person for the first time, making sense of a historical object and its importance, or figuring out the properties of a scientific phenomenon. Each of the dimensions of the visitor's lifeworld works in concert with the context of the object within the museum setting.

Dewey's concept of *transaction* (Dewey & Bentley, 1949) demonstrates this idea of the unity of subject and object from the outset, existing in one unified moment. Put more simply, in a transaction, the object and subject come together and merge rather than existing as two separate entities. This is different from Dewey's idea of interaction, which assumes the object and the subject are two equally balanced agents that meet but do not merge. Because the terms *interaction* and *transaction* have come to mean much more than these ideas, especially in museums, we frequently refer to visitor-object encounters and visitor-object intersections to denote Dewey's meaning of *transaction*.

Taken together these concepts of experience, unity, and transaction help describe the kinds of experiences that are possible in museum settings. In Chapter One, we explained the idea of consciousness. When a visitor has a unified experience with an object they become more and more conscious of the many ways that they can know an object. Not all unified experiences are deeply profound, but they satisfy visitors in some way.

As we described throughout this chapter, the Object Knowledge Framework draws on multiple theories and ideas about, and orientations to, the relationship between objects and people. The goal of the Framework is to begin new conversations about the ways museum staff can think differently about creating visitor experiences. In this model objects are not an afterthought, but are intentional components deeply entwined in the potential meanings and purposes of exhibitions and programs. Expanding our knowledge of the perspectives visitors bring to exhibition settings sheds new light on old practices. As museums are making transitions into new ways of thinking about visitors and the visitor experience, it is important not to leave the objects—and ways of thinking about objects—behind.

SECTION 2

Object Relationships

In this section we present research on person-object experiences in everyday life and in museums. Using three different research studies, we investigate the ways in which the lifeworld informs how museum visitors might encounter objects in the museum. Each of these studies sheds light on the many ways that people engage with objects in their lives both in and out of museums. By looking at person-object encounters in these various settings, we demonstrate how people attribute meaning to different kinds of objects and explore how those experiences might translate into a museum environment. Chapter Three provides deeper insight into personal identity and sense of being in the world that is connected to objects through individual narratives about childhood objects and then with museum objects. Chapter Four takes a look at how people create memories between each other and the past through objects. In particular the examples from research on a family museum illuminate the different meaning a collection of objects can have on a group. Finally, Chapter Five presents the deeply moving, "numinous" experiences and feelings of reverence that come from object encounters in museums demonstrating one type of unified experience.

CHAPTER THREE

Objects as Identity

Across the next three chapters we explore the unique relationships that people have with objects, both generally and in museum settings. We look at how people create identity, gain perspective, and come to revere objects through their interactions and personal connections with them. These personal connections to objects abound in every aspect of life, but because they are so ubiquitous, they may not always be apparent. Paying close attention to objects in everyday experiences is a useful way to see how people narrate their lives with objects and how those objects become part of their identity. In turn, this view provides valuable insight for curators and other museum professionals to see how museum visitors might encounter objects in a museum setting. The prior experiences, knowledge, and connections that visitors have with objects influence how they see an object in a museum (Doering & Pekarik, 1996).

There are countless examples of personal, meaning-laden objects in literature and film: the ring in *The Lord of the Rings*; Mike Mulligan's beloved steam shovel; the Velveteen Rabbit; the necklace worn by Rose in the movie *Titanic;* Rosebud, the famed sled from *Citizen Kane;* the box of military figurines in *Amelie;* and Wall-E's shelf of long-abandoned detritus of the 20th century. These objects and many others show how important object stories are in our daily lives. They become memorable because of the experiences people attach to them. Nearly every day, stories in popular media reveal the meaning of objects in people's lives. For example, in a recent *New York Times* health article, Abraham Verghese, M.D. ruminates on the meaning of the medical bag to doctors (2012). He describes the fascination he had when he first encountered the wonders of his uncle's medical bag, how it functioned as a portable medical office, and how his own bag now embodies the qualities of his mentor.

Elizabeth Wood and Kiersten F. Latham, "Objects as Identity" in *The Objects of Experience: Transforming Visitor-Object Encounters in Museums*, pp 58-71.

The ways people connect to objects make them valuable and meaningful; even mundane, "everyday" items can become vitally important in a person's life. Meaning-laden objects reflect and recount experiences and emotional connections: they reveal the lifeworld. The intellectual and emotional potential for learning from objects creates a broad base for meaning making to occur. In this chapter we take a close look at some everyday objects from childhood as a way to examine the interplay of the individual, group, and material dimensions of the Object Knowledge Framework. Then, we apply the same dimensions to stories about museum objects to show how people make connections to their identities in the museum.

Childhood Objects and Identity

The following three stories from adults about childhood objects illustrate the powerful ways that a person's individual, group and material dimensions (the lifeworld) intersect with the objectworld to form unified experiences. In all of these instances, the relationship between the object and the individual reveals an important story imbued with meaning and purpose. Though a museum visitor will not always see something of their own childhood in a museum, the kinds of person-object relationships demonstrated in the stories provide insight into ways that museums can transform object experiences around identity.

These narratives demonstrate the significance of childhood objects in relation to a person's identity in two key ways. First, objects are tangible possessions that help to signify a person's existence in the world: they are like containers that hold one's sense of being. They give a sense of protection, stability, and connection to other people. Second, when people use or touch an object, they feel they can move freely between their adult selves and their childhood selves—as though the object allows a person to exist across his or her own lifetime.

The particular objects described in these narratives are unique because of very specific markings or features that clearly, at least to the owner, make them distinctive. They are examples of *evocative* objects that reiterate the unifying life experiences that objects provide to human existence (Turkle, 2007). Whether they represent experiences of play, history and memory, or transitions and life passages, these objects make a clear statement in the telling of the owner's life stories. That personal connection is the catalyst for the unified experiences that museums strive to create.

The text included here of the narratives about a person's childhood object is selected and edited from conversations with Elee Wood (2005). To show how the Object Knowledge Framework works in these stories, the three lifeworld dimensions (individual, group, and material) described in previous chapters follow each narrative. This study of the different meanings of objects illuminates the powerful potential of the Framework.

Childhood Object Story: Anne's[1] Tablecloth

> My family's tablecloth was started in Christmas of 1958. My grandmother made it out of a plain length of green cotton material, with red rickrack around the edge. That first year it was a very plain, green Christmas tablecloth. What she had everyone do that year and every year since was to sign their name using a special pencil. I still have the same pencil that we've used since 1958. This is only time we ever use it. Everyone signed their name on the tablecloth, then she embroidered over that handwriting.
>
> Every year the ritual was the same. Sometime in the afternoon my mother would iron the tablecloth and put it out on the table. Then we kids would all race around the table trying to find our names on the tablecloth. Where am I in '62? In '63? Where am I in '64? We'd look around to find everybody else, grandma, grandpa, mom, and dad.
>
> Then, after supper, only when we're done with the meal, and after most of the dishes had been cleared, we could sign the tablecloth. We were always anxious, staking out the spot, trying to figure out a good spot. The kids always wanted to sign right away because it was just fun. Just trying to get a spot that would be visible and memorable was always important. There was a real ritual to it. The first time I signed the tablecloth would have been a sense of pride for me, I'm sure I did it as carefully as possible. It was such an important ritual to be able to do that and to be able to make my mark in the world. Even as I got older, it never became un-cool for me to sign the tablecloth. I always wanted to sign it. I always wanted to be there for Christmas. There's never been a time that I can remember any kind of teenager in my family saying, "Uh, I'm above this." Everyone signs every year because it is very real and very necessary to our family. This is very relevant to who we are, and I think all of us as teenagers understood that. It's because every year you get one shot at saying "I was here and I'm

1. All names are pseudonyms.

part of this." You're saying, "Yes, I belong. I belong to this family." There may have been times when I wished I belonged to a different family or wanted to break away, but on this one day we all knew that this is who we are, this is where we belong.

As a young adult, when I first moved away, there were a few years there where I didn't have a chance to be home for Christmas. Either we were in our own home, it was too snowy, or I was visiting my in-laws, or whatever it was. One of the biggest senses of loss of not being home at Christmas was knowing that I wouldn't be able to sign the cloth. That it wouldn't be just that moment that I wouldn't be there, but forever I wouldn't have been there.

When I look at this tablecloth it evokes memories for me of my family at this incredibly deep, visceral level in the same way that smells do for people. I think it really goes that far down in my brain stem. This isn't just cerebral cortex memories, these are really, really deep memories. It means more to me than anything. This tablecloth really evokes who I am.

Dimensions of the Tablecloth

As Anne's story unfolds, her observations and experiences demonstrate the interrelated dimensions of the Object Knowledge Framework. While she recognizes the material qualities of the tablecloth as a plain green cloth with red rickrack, the added description of the signatures changes the meaning. For her, this everyday item is far more than a simple tablecloth. The signatures and the stories about how those signatures came to be also reveal both the group and the individual dimensions of meaning.

The group dimension of Anne's story draws on familiar stories about family gatherings and rituals. The process of laying out the table and preparing the holiday meal provides more context and background for the experiences that Anne shares, but it is the very specific and very personal connection to the tablecloth that ties the experience together. Anne's connection to the tablecloth reflects her sense of self and identity. As she describes the individual meaning of the tablecloth, we see how the material and group qualities unite to create a deeply connected and moving relationship between a person and an object.

Having read the story of Anne's tablecloth, imagine an object from the *Art of Gaman*, a traveling exhibition on the arts and crafts of Japanese Internment camp prisoners (Hirasuna, 2005): a plain white handkerchief, signed by all the members of a cell barracks taken as a memento by a survivor of the camp. Each person's signature not only serves as a reminder of who was present in the barracks, but also evokes an important story about the lived experience of internment camps and a search for identity within American culture. Think about the stories that must exist within this museum object—those personal and individual stories connect with Anne's story in a very meaningful way.

Childhood Object Story: Jen's Ice Cream Scoop

I don't remember a time when we didn't have this ice cream scoop. It lived in the same place for almost 45 years, on the right-hand side of the drawer, on the right-hand end of the counter between the sink and the refrigerator. And, that's exactly where it was three years ago when we closed my parents' house and I took it.

The kitchen was one of the last rooms we cleared out. I remember opening that kitchen drawer, seeing the ice cream scoop. I flashed on myself as an 11 year-old kid with that ice cream scoop. If I were doing a movie with special effects, the ice cream scoop would have flown into my arms and cleaved to my breast. There was a bond and a connection between me and this silly utensil. I care really deeply about it. There was overwhelming emotion because I had assumed that my parents would have taken it with them to the new apartment.

I asked my siblings if anyone wanted it. Everybody clearly had their own memories with it, but nobody said, "No, you can't have it." My siblings kind of laughed about it. They said, "You know, it has no value, it's not like a beautiful thing like the china cabinet, and it's not an antique like great grandmother's china." To me it means my childhood. It just connects me right back to my parents' house.

When I hold the ice cream scoop, the house is right here around us. The counter is right here, the stove is over there. I'm at the table. I'm in it. I'm in the kitchen. I can smell things cooking, and I can see my mother. It's very immediate. My parents' kitchen was the center of life in our house. This ice cream scoop has a visceral connection to me as a kid. Even though I was the skinniest, the youngest, the one who got teased, I was also the one who got away with murder!

The feel of this ice cream scoop, the look of it transports me back pretty much completely into my mother's kitchen. It was a very safe, comfortable, loving place. It makes me feel all those things. It makes me feel safe and loved, like the world is very dependable. I even really don't care if

> I ever use it for ice cream, even though it is a very good ice cream scoop. It is somehow connected to this feeling of love and stability and reliability. Those things have been a really important part of me growing up to be who I am. That sense of love and stability and security are really what is strong in me, and I think the ice cream scoop is a part of that. It was all cooked up in that kitchen. That's where things happened. Good things and bad things.

Dimensions of the Ice Cream Scoop

We don't often imagine that a kitchen utensil could evoke identity, but this stainless steel ice cream scoop certainly does. Rather than serving as an example of 20th century kitchen gadget technology, the physical and tangible qualities of the scoop give context to the individual dimension. As Jen suggests, the sturdiness of the wooden handle and the manner of scooping ice cream remind her of family. The material nature of the ice cream scoop led Jen to "see" the kitchen and call up many family experiences and the way they shaped her life. The connections that she makes between her memories and membership in a family are intertwined with the activities related to ice cream.

In this object story many of the material qualities of the object become important links between the individual and group dimensions. In this narrative the ice cream scoop serves as a metaphor for the true meaning that Jen has with the object. It represents the solid, sturdy family connections and her sense of self. As a conduit to memory, this object exposes the ways that museums can link visitors to stories through material dimensions of an object. Rather than providing a specific description of an object's composition, various descriptors can evoke personal connections. Jen's use of the terms "stability" and "reliability" are reminders of feelings and experiences. Those descriptors can be useful in a museum exhibit. The more that the objects on display in museums draw out the interconnected nature of material, group and individual dimensions, the more visitors are able to make meaningful connections for themselves.

Building on the memories and associations that Jen has with the ice cream scoop and her family's kitchen allows us see the possible variations on the interpretation of a kitchen space. For example, the Smithsonian Museum of American History recreates Julia Child's Kitchen just as she left it. By displaying the collection of cooking utensils and the arrangement of her kitchen, visitors can see into the life of Julia Child, and likely many visitors relive the experiences of watching Julia Child on television or even think about their own cooking experiences. Similarly, in the British Museum's exhibition, *Life and Death: Pompeii and Herculaneum*, exhibition project curator Vanessa Baldwin describes the value of many of the artifacts as people's possessions that reveal their everyday lives and the value of learning something about who they were, how they lived, and what they did through their possessions (Trustees of the British Museum, 2013). This orientation to the individual dimension of household objects like windows, cooking utensils and chamber pots elicited many comments, blog and twitter posts from visitors.

Childhood Object Story: Katy's Blanket

> This is my baby blanket that I've had since before I was born. When I was about five the blanket was starting to fall apart and I remember sitting down with my mom and having this conversation that I should probably throw it away because it was so tattered. I was really, really upset and so instead, she agreed to put a new backing on it. I sat on the stairs right before I went to bed waiting for her to finish sewing the back on it because I couldn't go to sleep until it was finished. I was really scared that when she got finished with it, it wouldn't be the same thing anymore because it would have this new material on the back of it. It took days to break it in to feel the same.
>
> I took blankie with me to college and I came home at Thanksgiving and my mom took one look at it when I brought it home. She's like, "oh you've got to be kidding me. You know you're in college now, you might want to get rid of this." I didn't feel any less mature to have it, and I was away in the city 300 miles from home and if I wanted to keep something around that reminded me of that, then who was going to bother me? And so my mom and my aunts and my cousins all sat down in the basement and fixed it one more time. And they added this huge pink border, but specifically left open a little piece of the original fabric showing through. I think it was funny for them to fix it because it was this vulnerable piece of me and I thought it was really funny watching all of these women sitting in the basement—while the guys were watching football—fixing this baby blankie for this 19 year old girl.
>
> You know I think that blankie was just always this consistent thing. At first it was sort of something that I felt kept me safe in some way. And after awhile it became something I had to protect. I owed it something. Like I

remember when I was little sort of attributing emotions to it. You know like, I left it once at my aunt's house and I remember thinking that it was lonely. And then, even as old as like 6th and 7th grade, I left blankie for like 3 months, thinking that it was so silly that I'm thinking this inanimate object is lonely without me.

There are people in your life who traveled pretty far with you. But I think the thing about this is that it is one inanimate object that has traveled with me this entire time. Blankie is a map, I mean I can point to different pieces of it, and know where I was at a certain time. I can anticipate how much more it is going to deteriorate, or how to take care of it, or what I need to do.

Dimensions of The Blankie

Notions of safety and security are frequently associated with children's blankets and Katy's example is no different. As with other examples, the material dimensions of this blanket—colorful prints, story characters, etc.—are typical of quilts made for babies, something we imagine as part of the group dimension of this object. Katy's description of the feel of the material and how her mother added on to it help to show the personal connections to the physical dimension. Both the material and group dimensions contribute to a variety of connections that Katy can make to her childhood. The checkerboard pattern and blocks remind her of the landscape where she grew up, the well-worn fabric is soothing and comforting. When she was a child, the blanket absorbed her fears and worries and gave her a sense of protection.

These memories and feelings of care are often recounted in fiction and popular culture— perhaps most notable is the *Peanuts* character Linus. Such an understanding of the group dimension of blankets draws people in to remember their own blankets and the role these blankets played both in society and in their own lives. For Katy in particular, the individual dimensions of her blanket are like a map, almost like the checkerboard pattern of the fabric. She can see the stories and history of her life represented on each of the squares.

Similarly, artist Marie Watt explores the meaning of blankets in people's lives through her series, *Blanket Stories,* which has been exhibited in various art museums across the United States. The installations consist of towering columns of folded woolen blankets that bend and arch to evoke structural shapes. Watt's interest focuses on the blanket as an everyday function of human life and the many roles that blankets serve. She explores the personal connections that people have with objects, and particularly the ways that Native American groups use blankets as part of traditional gifts and honors. She describes the blankets as "being witnesses to important life events—births and comings-of-age, graduations and marriages, namings, and honorings" (Watt, 2011). In the same way that Katy's blanket calls to mind memories of land and family, Marie Watt's sculptural installations draw out the unique multi-dimensional roles that objects play in meaning making for visitors.

From Childhood Objects to Museum Objects

In these examples of objects from childhood, the stories reveal the lived experiences that the objects still represent to their adult owners. In each narrative, the encounter with the object helps to further extend an understanding of the lifeworld dimensions in the Object Knowledge Framework. Notably, the stories reveal the ways that experiences with objects reiterate John Dewey's description of an experience that has an aesthetic, emotional quality that unites and satisfies the individual. As Dewey (1916) writes:

> To 'learn from experience' is to make a backward and forward connection between what we do to things and what we enjoy or suffer from things in consequence. Under such conditions, doing becomes a trying; an experiment with the world to find out what it is like; the undergoing becomes instruction—discovery of the connection of things. (p. 164)

This connection of things—the relationship to the use and purpose of objects, the personal meaning of the objects, and the meaningful experiences with the objects—is the foundation of the unified visitor-object experience that museums can provide.

It is important to recognize that people can have the same kind of identity-related connections to museum objects as they do to personal or private objects. Keeping in mind the ways in which a visitor encounters an object in an exhibit is a key way to rethink how museum staff might transform their expertise into a meaningful connection with the individual. The objects of the museum are critical to making unified experiences happen; the preceding examples demonstrate that clearly. But the other crucial piece is the visitor's meaning making. The unified experience is possible when *both* the lifeworld and the objectworld intersect.

Personal stories about museum objects similar to those described in the preceding sections are not uncommon, but museum staff don't always get a chance to hear what visitors think about the objects in their museums. Fortunately, there are more and more efforts to make these personal connections both with the everyday objects that surround us and with museum objects. The following two examples give some insight into individual reactions to specific museum objects. These descriptions of encounters with museum objects provide perspective on the different meanings that objects can have and the way that unified experiences come about. The first uses the Object Knowledge Framework to describe an encounter with a museum object in an art museum. The second is an example of a museum project at the Portland Art Museum that highlights how the individual dimensions of the Object Knowledge Framework come to life.

Ere Ibeji (Male Twin Figures) from Stefanie's Perspective

Stefanie is a young museum professional who spent time during her college years as a docent at her university art gallery. Among her favorites in that collection was a set of figures carved from a single piece of wood representing human twins, called *ere ibeji*. During graduate school she served as a docent at the Indianapolis Museum of Art (IMA) and encountered a similar, but very different collection of *ere ibeji*. Seeing these figures at the IMA evoked a unified experience with the object that drew together her prior experiences with family and sense of identity. The following is Stefanie's description[2] of the *ere ibeji* using the dimensions of the Object Knowledge Framework.

> The first time I saw an *ere ibeji* was at the Ball State University Museum of Art. There were two figures in the case along with masks. They seemed small and out of place and I didn't understand their purpose. I forgot about them for a short time, until the museum launched a special exhibition of African art. During this exhibition a noted scholar came to speak about the collection and elaborate on the meaning of the items on display. She explained that the *ere ibeji* was a twin figure—a figure that houses one half of the shared soul of twin human beings. The Yoruba believe that twins share a soul, so when one twin dies half of the soul potentially goes with it endangering the living twin. To prevent this the *ere ibeji* is carved to house

2. Used with permission.

the half of the dead twin's soul to keep the living twin safe and the soul intact so that it can be reborn upon the death of both twins and live a full and long life.

This explained what the figures were, but they also left a great sadness in me, because while there were two figures, they were not matched—each was from a different set of twins. This means that somewhere, at one time there was a boy or a man who lost his brother. This figure was meant to keep him there with his twin, but instead it was locked away in a museum. Logically I knew that based on when the figures had been carved that the living twins they were attached to were likely dead themselves, but it still did not seem right that they had been separated.

I thought about the figures every now and then and made time to visit them. I moved away from Muncie two years ago and became a docent at the Indianapolis Museum of Art. One of the first galleries I wandered through was the African gallery; it has always been my favorite. It was there that I saw two shelves full of *ere ibeji* figures and for the first time I saw a pair. I knew that the pair represented twins who had both passed away and while their deaths made me sad I thought it was right that both figures be together. I do not hold the same beliefs as the *Yoruba.* I do not think that those individuals shared a soul and that a piece of wood can house that sort of energy or spirit. Yet, it seemed strange that these figures affected me so deeply. What was different about these two was that they had each other, they were complete. I did not feel the need to visit them because they were not lonely.

I have never really understood why I thought these figures needed me, but now I know why they mean so much to me. I don't believe in soul sharing or anything spiritual like that, but I do have a connection to my brother and sister, a connection that I have missed since I moved away. I'm originally from Fort Wayne and I moved to Muncie and then to Indianapolis to go to school. My parents divorced when we were all young and I took care of the younger two. Moving away means I missed almost all of my sister's teenage years and some of the landmarks of my brother's early adulthood. I have felt very guilty about that and wish there was a way I could be with them. The *ere ibeji* is a way for the Yoruba to connect to those who have gone, instead of being a marker of death they are a reminder of life and the connection of family. I don't think I'll ever get over the pain and guilt of being away, but the twin figures give me comfort in knowing my family is there.

In contrast to Stefanie's lifeworld experience, here are two dimensions of the *ere ibeji* objectworld from the museum's installation:

Material dimension: The museum catalog description:

Culture: Igbomina people.
Creation date: 1900-1950.
Materials: wood, pigment, glass, iron, fiber.

Group dimension: The museum gallery label (curatorial view):

The Yoruba have one of the highest rates of twin births in the world. Twins are believed to share the same soul and are generally considered to be a great blessing. They bring success to their family and cause harm to those who do not show proper respect. The mother will sometimes dance with them in public. Twins receive gifts and special meals, and enjoy much freedom during childhood.

Twins retain their power even after their death, and if one or both dies, the mother has a carver make a figure that serves to embody the spirit of the deceased twin. The mother treats it with the attention and respect any living twin deserves. She carries it with her, dances with it, feeds it, and adorns it with beads, cowrie shells and expensive cloth." (Indianapolis Museum of Art, 2012)

Personal and Museum Objects in Object Stories, Portland Museum of Art, Portland, Oregon

In this second set of examples on personal experiences with objects, we look at the Portland Museum of Art *Object Stories* project. As part of this project, visitors record stories and images of important objects from the museum or their own lives. The museum's goal is to invite visitors to explore "myriad ways objects speak to and shape who we are—our ideas, emotions, values, relationships, and aesthetics" (Object Stories, 2011c). The stories are both on display in the museum and categorized on a website according to a wide range of topics ranging from life experiences and relationships to personal connections to location, and an array of human emotions like joy, hope, courage, wonder.

The exhibit packs a powerful number of object stories into a small space. Visitors can watch and listen to recorded stories through the online database both on-site and at home, and can see objects as part of the on-going display. The intimate space highlights both stories and objects. Visitors may record their own stories in a nearby booth. The recorded stories reinforce the personal experiences that people have with objects. In the same way that personal objects evoke powerful feelings and experiences—clearly demonstrated through the stories the museum's visitors shared—the stories about museum objects hold a high level of personal connection. For example, one contribution about a woven basket tray begins with a knowledgeable description of its materials and form, as well as information about the weaver who made the basket (Object Stories, 2011a). These material details of the object, told by curator Dena Dartt-Newton, are interwoven with her own connections to tribal traditions and the need to share and maintain those with younger people. She goes on to describe seeing the basket in the museum as one that connects her, and "roots" her, to her homeland. Another example, from Ted Smith, one of the museum's security guards, begins by explaining his early encounters with museums in general (Object Stories, 2011b). The purpose of this explanation is to set the stage for his story about a handbag that he saw while on patrol in the museum. What's notable in his story is that the bag caught his eye because it looked like a bag he once owned. On further inspection, the bag itself was actually ceramic. Smith connects the encounter with his theories on life and art, and the role that museums play in looking carefully at things as a way of seeing "art" in life.

Staff at the Portland Art Museum (Object Stories, 2011c) provide visitors with a wide range of questions to stimulate ideas for the object stories. The prompts draw on key components found in the Object Knowledge Framework. In particular, these questions for visitors help draw out elements of the visitor lifeworld by asking about a time when they encountered the object, what it means, whether that meaning changed over time, how the object says something about the person, and how they learned the value or importance of the object. These strategies provide a strong link for the museum to support the significance that objects, whether personal or museum-based, hold for people's lives.

Identity Matters

The primary takeaway from these personal stories told about objects in everyday life and in museums suggests an important link between visitor and object that museums can support. In each of these examples the individual dimensions intermingle with the material and group dimensions, producing a unified experience. The personal connection each person makes to the object draws out fundamental aspects of identity and sense of being, sometimes unrelated to the actual object function. Yet, by seeing the kinds of meaning people attach to personal objects, we can begin to gain perspective on similar objects in museum settings.

If museums are to be places of relevance, then that relevance can come from the personal meaning that a visitor attaches to an object, as well as the group and material dimensions that the museum presents. That attachment might represent something that is part of the visitor's everyday world, or it may be a connection that develops through an encounter in the museum. In each instance, the intersection of visitor and object builds important layers of meaning and relationships between the person and the world around them. These connections create an important link not only to what the world is to us, but also to how it helps create who we are as people.

CHAPTER FOUR

Objects as Memories

Making individual connections to objects, like the childhood objects in the previous chapter, can result in significant unified experiences that ultimately lead to a greater sense of a person's identity and social connectedness. But the objects described in Chapter Three were personal possessions and the reactions to these objects were individual. In museum settings, objects must work for a great many people to provoke ideas, thoughts, emotions, or memories, or to reveal perspectives that a viewer may not see in another setting. In this chapter we focus on the way that people can have a variety of unified experiences with the same object or a collection of objects. We also look at specific approaches to displaying those objects that elicit different kinds of memories from a group of people. Using the Object Knowledge Framework, we illuminate the relationships between lifeworld and object-world, specifically around a collection of objects.

The research presented in this chapter is based on an emerging study[1] of family member experiences with objects in a place called "The Loft", a collection of more than 400 personal and local history objects located in a large room (roughly 375 square feet) above a family's garage in Maine. The Loft is best described as a family museum, but it is not publicly accessible. Gordon (2012) suggests that these kinds of "vernacular" museums demonstrate the "connectedness between consumption, history, individuality, and place… [and] allow people to discuss heritage without breaking from daily activities" (p. 76). The Loft mirrors these kinds of settings by providing an opportunity for intimate exploration of stories of the past and incorporating the layers of family history, culture, memory, and experience across multiple generations.

1. Family interviews from The Loft. Unpublished data collected by Elee Wood, 2013.

Jay is the owner of the space and the arranger of the collection. The Loft is Jay's personal space used primarily for relaxation during the day, but he often invites family and friends to visit in the evenings after dinner. Despite the fact that The Loft is not formally organized as a museum and is set in a non-museum space, the practices and experiences created there represent alternate ways to think about visitor-object encounters in more formal museum environments.

The Loft also provides insight into the function and role of intentional planning around objects. In general, museum collections are based on someone's ideas about what is important or special about a selection of objects: the collector, curator, or other museum staff constantly makes decisions about what the collection should (and should not) include within a set of parameters. The Loft is no different. There is a collection, a curator, a series of exhibits, and visitors. Just as in a formal museum, each visitor to The Loft must attempt to make sense of what they are seeing based on their own perceptions of material evidence, their collective group knowledge, and their individual connections. Most visitors to The Loft have a strong family connection to the objects in the collection, yet they have varying levels of individual experience with those objects. Thus the group dimension of each member's lifeworld is essentially developed around the family history (group understanding) of the object (material dimension), but each person's individual dimension reflects a somewhat different meaning. Just as in other examples we've presented thus far, where there are strong connections between visitor's lifeworld and object-world, there is a high likelihood for a unified experience to occur.

The Loft as a Museum

The Loft incorporates the material history of five generations of a single family and includes objects representing the local history of a small island where the family homestead is located. Although it is not open to the public, the extended family regularly visits this collection curated by "Papa Jay," head of the family. As the curator, he makes choices both about what goes into The Loft and when it is time for something to leave. He arranges things and provides interpretation. He decides whether each object has some historic meaning or connection to himself, his family, or the history of the property; sometimes though, he just keeps what he thinks is interesting or funny.

The Loft did not begin intentionally as a museum, but it has grown into something very much like one and has become very important to the family. "It just happened," Jay says, on the origins of The Loft. Through the process

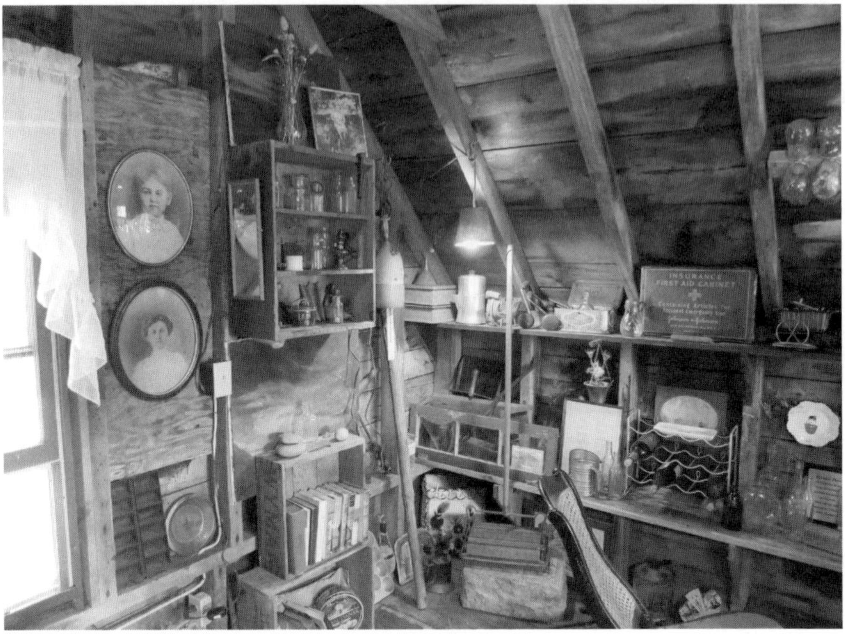

FIGURE 4.1 The Loft interior. Photo by Elee Wood.

of sorting and trying to make order out of his uncle's old carpentry shop, the source of The Loft's initial collection, Jay began to organize things into different displays, just for his own interest. Later he began to see how people responded to the space, and he created more opportunities to look at things: "I like to change things around, it's like a revelation. I like objects that might raise people's curiosity. … It's like penetrating beyond the obvious. You can kind of look at something and *then* try to imagine what era that came out of, who used it, how it was used."

Unlike the more traditional family collections displayed in curio cabinets and family rooms, The Loft has a distinctive and intentional feeling to it (Figure 4.1). There is evidence of deliberate organization and juxtaposition of objects, and a captivating array of exhibition-like technologies: strategies of mounting and hanging artifacts, cleverly placed lighting, hidden speakers, and comfortable seating.

Objects in the collection, like the "candlestick" bowling pins salvaged from the local bowling alley or old boxes and tools from the Wyman Blueberry farms, represent the island's history. There are examples of family history, including an array of photographs of family members, sleds belonging to Jay and his brother, carpentry tools from his uncle Yale, and a "Home Laundry" sign and washboard used by Jay's grandmother. There are also general (but authentic) examples of past domestic life including an old enameled kitchen table from the 1940s, canning jars, cooking and cleaning tools, and furniture from the family's homes in Los Angeles and Philadelphia. In addition to these historical elements, there is a sizeable assortment of artwork, much of which was done by members of the family. In short, the family museum is far more than just an assortment of collectibles or mementos. Jay's grandson, Pierce, suggested that *family* is imbued into everything in The Loft, that it is more a "museum of memories and people—not objects."

What these objects reveal is the family's collective, group identity, as interpreted through Jay's act of curation. Each of these possessions connects or relates to events and associations of the family members and family history. Each person can point to an object in The Loft and interpret their life events and memories through it. Family members also connect themselves to the history and continuity of the family and community context through their relationships to the objects. Although this museum is private (even family members can only visit by Jay's invitation), Jay's efforts in creating The Loft show a museum-like curatorial sense. There is an obvious set of displays for people to look at, the organization of materials makes a statement or inspires thought, and there is evidence of care and protection for the objects. These practices are a useful appraisal of how The Loft demonstrates the transformation of objects into significant opportunities for unified visitor-object experiences.

Examining Objects in The Loft

Whereas the childhood objects described in the previous chapter represent a singular personal experience with an object, family member experiences in the Loft provide examples of how different people experience the same object. At the same time, these encounters show how Jay's intentional shaping of the objectworld through his transformation of the objects creates memories for the family. A specific look at two objects in The Loft—a sofa and a bicycle—provides examples of the interrelated connections between a person's lifeworld and the objectworld within the Object Knowledge Framework. This view affords an opportunity to see how the meaning of objects changes across the family group and its individual members while simultaneously reflecting key aspects of the object's history and material qualities.

The Sofa

In The Loft, a majority of the family members interviewed mentioned one of the room's sofas as a significant object. This forty-year old floral sofa began as formal seating in the family's home in California, but years later they moved it to their new home in Philadelphia, where it became a casual piece of furniture in the family room. Eventually, Jay determined that the sofa should go to The Loft, where it remains today. In its current location, the sofa fulfills Jay's goals of creating a comfortable space for dialogue and reflection. Many family members recounted long hours of deep and open conversation while sitting on the sofa. Jay's nephew Jose Pablo said that in The Loft, the sofa has a "magical effect—it makes us talk." Indeed, while the sofa still serves a functional role for basic comfort and seating, the sofa itself prompts an array of memories for those who encounter it.

Even among the similar, shared descriptions of the group dimension of the sofa, each of the family members could just as easily describe a unique individual memory that was connected to it. Jay's daughters Samantha and Connie individually recalled silent reading time on the sofa with their mother. Jen, a close friend of the family, made an interesting connection to the sofa, explaining that even now, thirty years later, "the couch reminds me of Alicia's [Jay's wife] grandmother." Jose Pablo is continually reminded of singing holiday songs in Spanish for visiting family members. In each of these instances, the meaning of the sofa takes on the range of human emotions within the themes of family, love, and happiness.

Family members also reflected on the material dimensions of the sofa, noting the functional and stylistic aspects. They quickly identified its age and "fashion from another time." Certainly this 1970s era floral sofa is a thing of the past; yet, at the time that most of the family initially encountered it, they recall the sofa was an important piece of furniture for entertaining guests. Then, and now, they describe the sofa as a comfortable place to sit, to converse, and even to sleep. Kent, Jay's second son, explained that the sofa has functioned like a "spine" where "family is the common denominator."

The mix of lifeworld experiences and memories with the sofa through the individual, group, and material dimensions is not necessarily unique to The Loft. In their study on cherished household things, Csikszentmihalyi and Rochberg-Halton (1981) identified forty-one different categories of meaningful objects ranging from broad descriptions (e.g., televisions and sports equipment) to specific (e.g., trophies and collectibles). Among the objects most frequently mentioned, and most beloved, across three generations was furniture—sofas, chairs, and tables. The study's participants noted these functional objects of everyday life not because of their utilitarian nature, but because of their representation and embodiment of memories and experiences, and as signs of self and family. Looking at the experiences with the sofa in both studies provides insight into the ways that something as potentially mundane as seating and furniture might elicit meaning from visitors.

The Bicycle

Tucked under a tall workbench in the Loft is a child's bicycle. The Loft's bicycle, a 1960s, red Schwinn Pixie, represents a milestone that each member of the family had in learning to ride a bicycle. According to Alicia, "it's part of our history." Many family members commented on the significance of moving the bicycle with the family from Los Angeles to Philadelphia, and how it was handed down to each member for the important rite of passage. The shared group knowledge of this bicycle stems not only from each member's own experience with it, but also from seeing others in the family learn to ride.

This specific bicycle has "traveled through all the kids' lives," according to Samantha. It started in California as a birthday present for Jay Jr., then the family moved it to Philadelphia where both younger siblings and the neighbor children learned to ride. Later they took it to Maine for summer vacations, where it ultimately began its new role in The Loft, no longer something to be ridden but a representation of memories past. In an amusing recounting of the ownership of the bicycle, each family member describes their memory just a bit differently, and in each instance, the history of the bicycle is not independent of the viewer but is instead recreated into each of their own respective histories. The bicycle didn't just belong to one child or the other: it belonged to each one not only as *theirs* but also as something that was part of the family. Alicia, Jay's wife, explained, "My father bought it for our oldest son Jay—in California. It was the first bike we ever had. And that bike, all our kids learned to ride that bike." Connie, the youngest daughter, said, "I don't remember learning how to ride the bike. I remember being told we all learned how to ride [on it] . . . but I remember that being my bike." Jennifer, a friend of the family said, "I learned to ride on that red bike. They had a long driveway, and they had a blacktop, and that's where I learned how to ride, on that bike."

The story of the family bicycle presents an interesting look at the role of personal, group, and material dimensions of the bicycle. Certain dimensions become important elements of the ways that each family member connects to it. Unique physical features like the multiple "STP" stickers on the fender help some family members connect the bicycle to their own histories, and in turn, the history of the bicycle within the family centers around each person individually. Notably, no one in the family ruminated on the design or particular significant historical details of the bicycle itself. They did, however, consider it in terms of what it meant to learn how to ride a bike and the memories and feelings associated with it.

What seems unique about the bicycle in The Loft is that Jay makes no attempt to place it in any particular time or place in history outside of the family, as it might be if it were in a more formal museum. Similarly, while the size and style of a bicycle, features such as the slope of the frame or the height of the handlebars, might communicate information about its use, none of the family members explain the importance of the bicycle in this way. That particular, structural, knowledge of bicycles is not important for this setting. Instead, the ways that the family members know this object is through their lifeworld connections and the shared knowledge of how the family used the bicycle over time.

In the two preceding object examples, the types of memories evoked by the sofa and the bicycle reflect the way that the individual, group, and material dimensions of the lifeworld contribute to meaning making. Even though members of the family draw from a shared group experience, they each have a different orientation across all three dimensions. The objects evoke memories across time and place, often starting in The Loft, but taking each person back in time to another place where they used the object. Similarly, the objects evoked memories of people and events and served more like a conduit or a starting point for the memories.

Linking Object and Person through Assemblages

As the curator of The Loft, Jay recognizes his role as a transformer of the objects. He sees his goal as one that stimulates looking and thinking. He arranges things in particular ways with the intention to spark some kind of curiosity and revelation and, as he says, "to penetrate beyond the obvious." He achieves this by displaying the objects in clever ways, often through unique assemblages that echo the ideas of the cabinet of curiosity—an archetypal example of the earliest museums where many different kinds of objects would be displayed all at the same time. Jay deliberately creates artistic juxtaposition and positioning of objects so that they will be seen in certain ways. In fact, were The Loft's exhibits to have a "big idea," it may well be a revelation of the meaning of family and home, past and present. Jay's goal in creating the experience of the Loft is very intentional: "Everything has some historic meaning or connection to myself. It can't go, it has to stay.... I don't want [my family] to be forgotten. I want everyone to know whose home this is." The goal of using the objects to preserve the memory of family is very clear. Every member of the family interviewed during this study was quite adamant (and emotional) in their recognition that this museum was indeed a deeply-rooted interpretation of the family.

Even without didactic text panels or messages, Jay creates the memory of home and family through a multi-layered process that draws together elements of the objectworld and connects with people's lifeworlds. Jay is not trained in museum practices, but his instincts about creating displays and vignettes draw out the revelatory results he desires. Two major approaches make the visual story of The Loft come to life: first, it is genuinely historical without being chronological. Looking at the space itself, every inch of the walls (and much of the ceiling) contains a cross-section of family history and story. Nothing is linear. Old and new stories co-exist through the creative juxtaposition of objects. For example, propped up along one wall is an old wooden sled with wooden runners that extend beyond the base. Nestled in the curvature of the sled runners, Jay has placed a modern, floral patterned cookie tin. Hanging to one side is a basket of dried flowers; a rusty fox trap hangs on the opposite side. The visual composition of this "installation" draws attention to each of the objects and at the same time invokes potential stories.

In another exhibit in The Loft (Figure 4.2) Jay mounted a metal meat grinder on top of a wooden box. Inside the box are small jars and blocks of wood. Inside the meat grinder is a vase of dried flowers and a collection of skeleton keys hangs off the front. On top of the box is a pair of barber shears and a straight razor. Embedded within this display are the stories around the razor and Jay's first experience learning to shave:

> Uncle Yale's razor... what's it say, I can't read it, uh... Crowns and Sword Razor Works. Wahl, Germany. This little razor, he used every day. Man, he had a really rough beard. When I was a teenager, I took this out once, and I looked in the mirror, and I went three times [motioning up and down his cheek], and I made three cuts on my face! So I put that immediately away, and I never used it again, but I'll never forget it. It's when I was young, you know, when you're a young boy, you wanna be—you wanna *shave*.

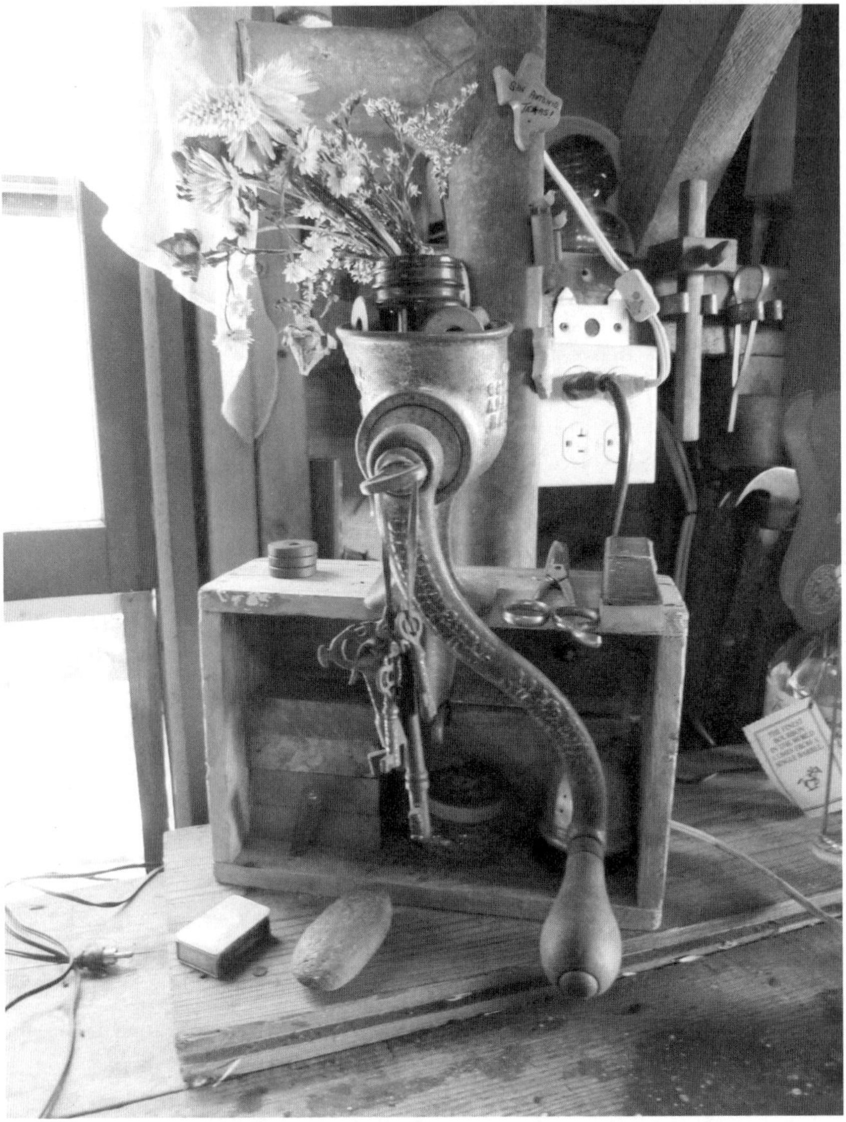

FIGURE4.2 An object assemblage in The Loft. Photo by Elee Wood.

The second important approach that brings life to Jay's Loft exhibits is that they are thematic without being categorical. Rather than grouping all of the cooking items together, or all of the woodworking tools in one place, Jay has distributed them around The Loft. Just as the space draws on cross-historical elements, the themes in The Loft cut across ideas like boating, travel, entertainment and merriment, labor, hospitality, food and drink, and functionality. Generally Jay combines objects for their aesthetic elements, but in some instances they are connected by Jay's personal stories and in others by shared family stories and history. Near the stairs, a series of small buggy wheels and ice skate blades sit between the wall joists (Figure 4.3), framed by long carpenter levels. Two ink drawings, also set in between the wall joists, complete the overall look. The clever integration of the physical elements of the walls, along with the shape of the wheels, the skates, and even the paintings presents a striking visual image that again draws attention to each object individually, as well as the composition as a whole. These approaches help draw out the viewer's sense of curiosity, as well as the important aspects of historical and family revelation that Jay seeks.

Clearly, the range of memories associated with each object is what makes The Loft important to the family. However, interviews with close friends and extended family who have visited The Loft demonstrate that there are more than just family connections to the space. Non-family members are equally intrigued by the way that Jay displays the objects, and are drawn to the history of both the family and the surrounding island towns. The orientation and positioning of the objects historically without being chronological, and thematically without being categorical highlight elements of the objectworld beyond the material dimension. These connections to elements of the objectworld, whether direct or implied, help to bridge the meaning between object and person and often result in the kind of unified visitor experience with objects that makes museums powerful.

Jay's role as the curator in The Loft is certainly based on his direct link to the objects in the collection. However, despite this connection, he realizes that each object means something different to people who visit The Loft. Maria, one of Jay's nieces, described all of the objects, as *significant*: "they had a life, now they are here, they are not ornaments." At the same time, Jay's goal is not about preservation of the objects, but preservation of the experiences. The objects themselves help to facilitate those experiences, but without him and others, they are without meaning. In this sense, Jay understands that without the lifeworld to activate the meaning, the objectworld is far less important. Jay recognizes that in the end, the objects are not themselves the memories, but the transaction between the person and the object. When thinking about what might happen to The Loft contents, Jay says:

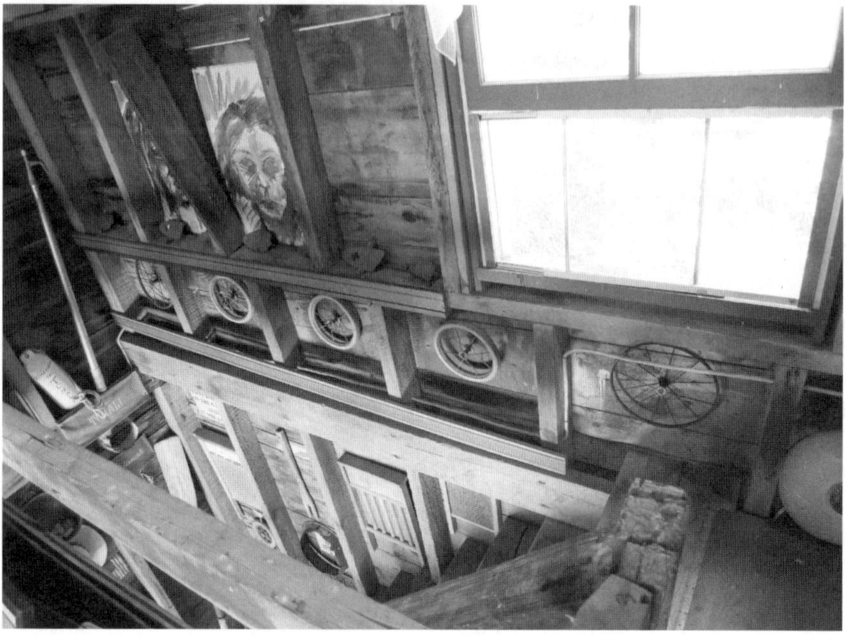

FIGURE 4.3 Integration of varied objects. Photo by Elee Wood.

> Who would want this old sifter over there for flour? I don't know who would want that. Is that more important than that little pie pan over there? Give me a break! I say you either gotta take it down and give whatever has any significance to the some other museum or library or whatever, take it to the antique fair, and see if we can get twenty-five cents for something. I don't see what you could do with it.

From The Loft to the Museum

The opportunity to study and document family museums like The Loft offers an important avenue for better understanding the relationships that museums can build between visitors and objects. Lying beneath the surface of this family museum is calculated and purposeful storytelling drawn from local and familial histories. At the same time, The Loft portrays, even if on a small scale, the role played by curators and exhibit planners in facilitating the translation of the objectworld into something meaningful to a visitor's lifeworld. Such an approach intentionally incorporates the life experiences and visions of many more contributors than the museum professionals putting it together; it also represents inclusive, visitor-driven narratives that incorporate meaning and perspective across multiple facets of life (See for example Adair, Filene & Koloski, 2011; Henry & McLean, 2010; Wood, 2009). Jay is the expert on the space and the things contained in it, but he is not worried about his visitors taking away his meaning: he wants them to think and look, wonder with curiosity, and draw from it what they will.

What can museums learn from The Loft? Creating a moment of revelation or building opportunity to make a memory is a great way to think about the role of objects in an exhibition or a program. Sometimes that means providing context for the object—beyond simple identification labels—in some form of immersive environment like a diorama, installation, or assemblage. Or it might mean taking away distracting information, simplifying the presentation of the object. The act of planning how the visitor sees and experiences the objects is part and parcel of what helps to create the unified visitor-object experience.

The Object Knowledge Framework emphasizes the importance of offering multiple viewpoints to the visitor. There is more to the story of an object than meets the eye. Visitors in museums may not have all the deeply shared knowledge of a family or even a specific history of an object; instead, the connections that people make have to come from the different ways that the museum transforms that knowledge of the objectworld into an exhibition or program. Visitors who are able to access the stories and unique events connected to an object develop a greater appreciation for the meaning and purpose that it holds. The importance of an object itself does not diminish in the face of personal connections; rather, these aspects of the object's own story help to bring out connections to larger ideas and experiences.

CHAPTER FIVE

Objects as Reverence

Chapters Three and Four provided insight into the kinds of relationships that people have with objects in a range of settings outside of formal museum spaces. In this chapter, we explore the meaning of the Object Knowledge Framework as it pertains to visitor experiences in more formal museum settings and historic sites. In the museum context, many visitors, staff, and scholars refer to the powerful, almost sacred nature of some exhibition spaces, experiences, and objects. Nelson Graburn (1977), now somewhat famously, called these types of museum experiences "reverential" and part of "the visitor's need for a personal experience with something higher, more sacred, more out of the ordinary than home and work are able to supply" (p. 13). He characterized this experience as something of magic, fantasy, and sacredness and considered the experience to be personal and private, a "solitary one of contemplation, meditation," filled with the "freedom to fantasize and make connections" (p. 14).

Many museum professionals experience this kind of powerful reaction to museum objects or exhibits. In the 1990s researchers investigating the "pivotal" museum learning experiences of museum professionals found that participants told profound stories about early museum experiences. They recounted vivid recollections that opened possibilities for broader life horizons, and elicited strong, deeply felt and long-remembered emotions (Spock, 2000). The researchers reported that many of the stories involved a museum object. In many cases, the object experience sparked a life change, or a shift in perspective that eventually led to the role the person held at the time of the interview.

Examining the "Numinous"

Interested in similar connections, anthropologists Catherine Cameron and John Gatewood (Cameron & Gatewood, 2000, 2003; Gatewood & Cameron, 2004) wrote a series of articles describing the *numinous* experiences visitors had at historic museums and sites. Broadly defined, a numinous museum experience is a meaningful, transcendent experience that results in a deep connection with the past. Cameron and Gatewood borrowed the term *numen* from religious philosopher Rudolf Otto's book, *The Idea of the Holy* (1917/1965). The numinous, according to Otto, contains a "moment" that is almost inexpressible in normal terms and concepts. Numinous consciousness is a state of mind, and is in the same category as one's reaction to "the beautiful." It is a qualitative feeling or affect, but also more than that. The numinous cannot be taught, only awakened or evoked in the mind of the person, and "can only be suggested by means of the special way in which it is reflected in the mind in terms of feeling" (Otto, 1917/1965, p. 12). The numinous is endowed with transcendence, majesty, and an overpowering sense that goes beyond any created thing and is also beyond the familiar, the usual, or the intelligible (Lopez, 1979).

Cameron and Gatewood (2000, 2003; Gatewood & Cameron, 2004) used this concept to explore the underlying motivations of tourist visits. "Why else," they asked, "beyond information-gathering, having fun, and creating family memories, do people go to historic places?" They hypothesized that people often seek a deeper, more meaningful connection with a place or time period—a bit more akin to a spiritual quest—and they called these people *numen-seekers*, offering a non-religious context for this response. Historic sites and displays, they hypothesized, can conjure in visitors a visceral or emotional response to an earlier event or time, one that could allow them to achieve a connection with the "spirit" of the times or people of the past. In their description of the phenomenon, Cameron and Gatewood refer to Csíkszentmihalyi's (1990) work on "flow" and cite another study on tourism that describes this kind of experience as a cognitive state "in which there is intense engagement, a loss of the sense of time passing, and a transcendence of self" (Prentice, Witt & Hamer, 1998, p. 3). In their studies on visitors to historic sites in Bethlehem, Pennsylvania, and Gettysburg National Military Park, Cameron and Gatewood found that 27% of visitors surveyed were "numen-seeker types," that is, the visitors were actively seeking some sort of personal experience with historic sites and museums. The authors then tentatively suggested three dimensions that make up the numinous museum experience: (1) deep engagement or transcendence, (2) empathy, and (3) awe or reverence.

These reverential, spiritual, or even awe-inspiring encounters in museums should lead museum staff to ask what is going on with these experiences and envision how they can help people have them more often. As way to explore the reverential experiences a person may have with a museum object, we will look at a specific study of numinous experiences in museums. The rest of this chapter is devoted to digging a bit deeper into these profoundly emotional experiences that people have with objects in order to highlight some of the elements of the Object Knowledge Framework.

Taking it One Step Further: Numinous Experiences with Objects

In 2009, Kiersten Latham conducted a study built upon this pivotal research in which museum visitors from five history and art museums were interviewed about their deeply felt experiences with museum objects. Analysis of the interviews revealed four characteristics of these experiences: unity of the moment with the object, the nature of the object as a link to the past and others, a feeling of being transported, and making connections bigger than the self. These four core characteristics of the encounter are not mutually exclusive elements. They tend to follow the characteristics Cameron and Gatewood proposed, but build on them in important ways. The holistic model of unity that came out of Latham's analysis was derived directly from museum visitors' descriptions. The resulting interpretation attempts to underscore the many layers of the experience with a museum object: a person encounters the numinous simultaneously at many levels—intellectual, emotional, imaginative, sensual.

Numinous Experiences with Museum Objects

In this section, we introduce the people who participated in this study, explain each characteristic of the numinous experience in more detail, and provide actual quotes from each of the participants that ground the features of these encounters with objects. To help contextualize the characteristics of the experience, it helps to get to know the study participants and the objects they spoke about. The following is a brief introduction to the five people—two men and three women—whose interviews were analyzed in this study and the main objects and museums they talked about.

Annalise talked about two sets of objects: paper cutouts by Matisse at the Detroit Institute of Arts, and an oil painting at the Louvre. Her experiences began at age nine and continued through college. She was a volunteer at the Detroit Institute of Arts at the time of the interviews.

The main artifact Erin spoke about is a Renoir painting at the Museum of Fine Arts in Boston. She was college age when the encounter occurred. When interviewed, she was an educator at a living history museum.

Most important to Mary was the chair Lincoln was sitting in when he was assassinated, held at The Henry Ford in Dearborn, Michigan. She also spoke a bit about a boarding house in Williamsburg, Virginia. Both encounters occurred when she was an adult. Mary was a third grade school teacher at the time of the interview.

Phil's encounter occurred at Gettysburg National Military Park, in Pennsylvania, on Little Round Top hill, with a tree and a photograph from the time just after the Battle of Gettysburg. His experience occurred right after he had graduated from military college, gotten married, and was on his way to his first officer job. Phil was a volunteer at the National World War I Museum in Kansas City, Missouri, a retired Army officer, and taught high school math when this study was conducted.

Around age ten, Richard had his encounter with the Lincoln chair at The Henry Ford in Dearborn, Michigan. Richard taught high school science and was acting as his school's leadership activities sponsor when he was interviewed.

The stories from these five participants provide illustration of the thematic concepts that constitute a numinous museum experience: unity of the moment with the object, the object as a link, a feeling of being transported, and making connections bigger than the self.

Unity of the Moment

Unity of the Moment refers to the holistic and dynamic experience that occurs between person and object during a numinous encounter. It is the overarching quality of the experience, the sphere in which the other three characteristics occur. When participants talked about their moments, they tended to describe them as dynamic, "vivid," and with great detail. As the elements united in each person's experience, sudden moments of clarity occurred. These experiences had an enduring effect on each person, as exemplified by their descriptions of connections that transcend memory, time, and self.

Unity of the Moment is not a connection flowing through the experience: it *is* the experience. Participants used language that revealed the encounter as something distinct, something different from other experiences. One person called it "interfacing" and another summarized the encounter as one where "all things kind of align together." Richard repeatedly called his boyhood experience of Lincoln's chair "my moment" to describe his numinous experience. His moment was grand, deep, and involved his intellect and experiences as well as his emotions and feelings. Wrapped up in the story of his moment are his identity, his family, his career, and the bigger questions of national pride and the meaning of life.

Object Link

In the *Object Link,* the object plays a significant role during a numinous encounter in its tangible, physical form as well as in its symbolic form. In its tangible form the object is a trigger or link to something: it sparks the perceptions, thoughts, and/or feelings in this encounter, or acts as evidence or a witness to the past. It begins the experience; the immediacy of the object's existence starts the numinous reaction. According to participants, the object's physical presence helps bring "it" to life; "it" may be history, people, or actions, but is always something that can be real. As Mary says, seeing Lincoln's chair "brings all the things from the printed page that I've had the pleasure of reading over the years alive at that moment when I'm viewing the item." Phil also described it this way when he saw the tree and photograph at Little Round Top:

> ... it brings history home, it makes history alive. I've read about this for years, but I'm standing on the spot where it actually happened. And it's like earth-shattering and I'm seeing evidence that was during the battle is still here.

Because of its physicality, or three-dimensional nature, the object has become a "witness to history," representing events and people of the past and bringing them in to the present. In addition, Erin often spoke of the object almost as a living being. She described the Renoir painting as "speaking to" her, "calling" her, and talking about the person in the picture as a familiar friend.

The person's proximity to the artifact or the need to touch it is another element of the tangible object as a link to the past. All participants imagined touching the objects they described, citing this as an important way to get "into" its history or past. Erin had the strongest need to touch the Renoir painting she talked about.

> ... feeling that somehow—and I knew better not to—but if I could touch the painting, you know that feeling of "huh" [air inspired quickly], maybe I'll touch the spot that nobody else has touched since Renoir put the paint there, just that feeling of, I'm gonna find it.... It was just that overwhelming sense that if I could just touch this, that I would be touching—that the hundred years would slip away and—I felt I knew him just by looking at what he had done.

Richard thought if only he could sit in the chair, the experience would have been even more intense:

> Well, I think it would have been even more powerful just because I think that would have been like, the ultimate of that experience.... Here I am in the exact same chair that Abraham Lincoln got shot in and... that would like literally be being part of history.

Despite the clear sense of the tangible, no one actually touched the object central to each of his or her encounter.

In its symbolic form, the object was a kind of receptacle, holding meaning far deeper and more profound than its simple function or features. In fact, the object, at times, embodied grand symbolic meanings for the person about larger issues such as death, patriotism, or the meaning of life. For example, Richard felt Lincoln's chair "contained" more than just a place to sit or even a place where a man was killed. To him it symbolized the "what-ifs" of history and the big issues of the Civil War. Mary, who talks about the Lincoln chair, says it well:

> As solid as that chair is when you look at it—it's solid, it's carved, heavy carved wood—and a very bold and courageous man sat in that and he really withstood a lot and went through such a tough time in our history, and was a good man and I think that chair embodies—I never thought of it before but as I'm explaining—that chair embodies a lot of what I feel is important in life and a lot of what I think our country has been and has stood for.... I look at that chair, for whatever reason, it just embodies, it just embodies Lincoln and that period and what was going on and that's how it comes to life for me. That reaction with that chair is just really different for me.

Being Transported

The characteristic of *Being Transported* shows that the numinous experience affected people in ways beyond the cognitive. Being Transported involves elements of time, space and body; participants felt time and space alter and physically reacted to the encounter through their body.

Time. During a numinous experience with a museum object, the description of what happens to time is very consistent among all of the participants. They described time as slowing or stopping. Phil says he felt like he was frozen in time during his encounter. Annalise describes time as "standing still," saying, "I think that's when time stopped that day, and I could just take a breath and life was good again." In addition, people often described themselves as "being transported back in time." Phil described his encounter at Gettysburg, "... like being in a time machine, and dialing the date back to July, 1863, and 'being there!'" Even today, Mary feels "transported" whenever she sees the chair.

Time also seems to compress or feel very recent regarding the experience. Phil felt like the episode, which occurred in 1975, felt "like it happened yesterday." During her interview, when asked how long she stood there looking at the Matisse cutouts, Annalise said, "I don't know. I'm still ... standing there ... in my 40s, so probably 30 years I've been standing there."

Space. The characteristics of lived space in the numinous encounter include a sense of movement, "tunnel vision," and the impression of being alone. Participants describe their vision narrowing or focusing and forming a "tube" or tunnel between themselves and the object or exhibit. The edges of their vision blur, darken or fuzz out and the object is highlighted, illuminated, or details are enhanced. Within this sensation, they describe moving toward or away from the object. Annalise, in her encounter with the nativity scene in the oil painting, said she felt like she was being pulled away from the painting. Erin also speaks of the movement and the illumination of the painting:

> ... in TV shows you know sometimes they do that camera trick where the person's being, something's being sucked towards the person, the camera? That's kind of what you felt. I mean, I felt ... like I was being drawn to it. Or drawn into it.... As I'm looking backwards on it, I can see [the painting] framed in the doorway and I'm sure there was a light hanging right over it—everything else was dark except for this painting.

Richard said the space around him and Lincoln's chair got smaller and darker: "It was like one of those movie moments where the lights dim out and ... you're standing there and ... it's you and the thing. Everything got more enhanced, I could see the detail better on the Chair."

Phil said that the Little Round Top photograph and tree "captured him":

> It's kind of like there's nothing else around, you're just focused on that. It's kind of like you're lookin' through a paper tube, or something ... like that's the only thing that's on your attention, or, captures your attention.... It kind of freezes you in time and everything else that could be a distractor goes away and you're just focused on this for three seconds and you wish it lasted longer. But during that three seconds there, you're just so focused.... Everything else in the museum ... it fuzzes out ... you're just focused on this one thing for three seconds.

In his description, Phil mentioned there being "nothing else around" and others describe the sense that people around them have disappeared, real or not. While in the very crowded, blockbuster (her description) Matisse exhibit, Annalise said, "It's like all the people disappeared." Mary said similar things happened with Lincoln's Chair:

> It feels like I'm alone in the room; it doesn't matter how many other people are there.... And again, I can be walking with other people but it's a very one-on-one-experience, for me at that moment. Even though there might be a crowd and you're moving along quickly....

Lived Body Lived body refers to how the person physically felt during the experience. Everyone except Erin described physical sensations from the encounter. Annalise felt numbed, and Richard said he felt "odd." Phil described his experience as a "rush," "blood rushing to your face," and said that just talking about it brought the rush back. "It's a tingling sensation, mostly in my face, but I'd say my upper body too and seriously, I've had it four times just talking here as I bring these emotions up." Mary describes it as "total tingly excitement," and felt "butterflies":

> ...it's as though for that few minutes that I'm exposed to that artifact that I literally can picture, I can feel, just it's almost like a physical feeling.... I remember lingering and just *looking* at it and literally—this may sound strange but—literally, feeling the butterflies, literally feeling a physical reaction.

Connections Bigger than Self

In the fourth theme, *Connections Bigger than Self*, participants all speak of "connecting" to something, whether it be the object, the historic past, their personal past, or something higher in life. Richard, for example, said, "It felt different...there was definitely a connection there between me looking at this thing" (the chair) and spurred him to think about "where I've gone, where I've been, what I'm doing here, how I've been there." He believes there is an "attachment" between him and the chair that continues today. For Erin, seeing the painting gave her a connection to the past, to the artist, and to her childhood. "I can see the brush strokes and picture the artist's hands at work, and I truly felt transported to his time and connection with him that seemed to me almost eternal." These connections are about the person's existence in this world, about who they are and why they are here. They help the person understand things about themselves and their relationship to the world around them. Participants made *connections* in three areas:

1) with their *reflective self* and sense of being, purpose, and relation; 2) with people of the past whom they have never physically encountered but are able to connect through *imaginative empathy*; and 3) with *higher things*—the more spiritual phenomena of reverence, awe, and meaning of the larger things in life.

Reflective Self This part of the theme refers to the profoundly meaningful personal connections (about the self) made during the experience with the object. This connection was extremely meaningful to each person, having a lasting effect, and for some, dramatically altered or influenced their lives. For most, it affected their career choices and path in life. For all, the numinous experience with a museum object was wrapped up in personal identity, with family and in life-defining moments. Mary said of her experience with the Lincoln chair, "If that chair had not been there…I really believe I would be a different person today." Phil, whose experience was at Gettysburg Battlefield site, professed that the encounter at Little Round Top was an epiphany. It helped him see his place in the world: the experience "dinged him" and "ignited his soul." It changed his whole understanding of his role as an Army officer. Before the encounter at Gettysburg, he had been somewhat complacent about his career:

> I think, this [visit to Little Round Top]—more than the four years I spent in training—did more to ignite my soul into embracing this career of a… professional officer in the army, than anything else.… And I think I carried that. You know, it's like, hey, this is serious business—the tradition of being in the United States Military.

Erin, who was "overwhelmed with emotion" upon seeing the original painting by Renoir in Boston, also felt the experience was very personal, seeing the painting that day was like "unearthing a treasure" and she had the sense that the painting was put there just for her. She called the painting "hers" and that "everyone else could look at it but it was really mine." She strongly associated the painting, which she had purchased a copy of as a 9-year-old girl, with her identity.

Imaginative Empathy While the definition of empathy is "a sense of shared experience, including emotional and physical feelings, with someone or something other than oneself" ("Empathy" 2009), *imaginative empathy* involves an active conjuring of an empathic moment. The participants in this study connected beyond simple empathy; they seemed to be trying to bring forth images and personalities of people and events they had not experienced in their own lives. There was a real sense of them actively trying to pull, or extract, stories and personal feelings of the distant past out of the objects. Referring to the people from the historical past, Phil said, "it's like I was a part of something that these people were there before me." Mary, describing an experience in a Williamsburg boarding house, said:

> The places where real people that you studied about and read about used to actually pay their couple of cents, and sleep up there in the crowded conditions, sharing beds and not taking baths and all that stuff. The visualization that a real person sat in *that* chair or slept in *that* bed or was drinking ale in *that* tavern with the pewter mug and the plates ... it just—the only way to say this—it just POPS it right out at me and, I'm just excited even talking about it.... I think it's like, at that moment I think, what if I was the fly on the wall and I was there observing. It brings it to life—from the pages. And it brings it, in a sense, to life for me, like I can really picture what it might have been like to literally live at that time.

Erin, talking about Renoir's actual model for the painting, said: "She was a real person too.... Here I am looking at all this a hundred years later. I'm looking in the face of a real live girl, seeing the brushstrokes.... And it started with a simple painting." Erin likened the experience she had with the painting to a connection across time, which she compared to the symbolism in the Sistine Chapel imagery:

> You know the only thing that comes to mind is the hand of God reaching down and touching Moses, I mean that sense of a hand reaching across time and touching you. I'm not trying to be blasphemous in saying that God and Renoir are the same but it's that image of a hand reaching out from the past and touching you.

Higher Things. The concept of "higher things in life" (Kari & Hartel, 2007) refers to "usually positive human phenomena, experiences, or activities that transcend the daily grind with its rationality and necessities" (p. 1133). In particular these experiences are *profound* higher things, regarded as deep and sublime. In Latham's study, this element is characterized by connections that are reverential, full of awe, spiritual, deeply meaningful, and extraordinary. Often participants described epiphanic moments—sudden realizations of the meaning of something. Annalise describes her feeling about the Matisse paper cutouts, "I can't put a word on it ... it was something awesome." While comparing her experience with someone she witnessed having the same experience, Erin called it a "coming-to-Mecca sort of thing." In describing her encounter with the painting, she said:

> Oh, wonderful! I mean ... it was just a very emotional; and ... it was almost sanctuary-like, Sunday morning, it was quiet; it wasn't very busy at the museum. And it was a very personal, sort-of spiritual experience, kind of touching that core of you. As I said, I'd always studied in a very intellectual way and thought of it as, "I'm smart, I know about painting." But, to look at it in that very spiritual way. ...

Mary believed Lincoln's chair brought out her love for her country and her realization of how lucky she and others are to be a part of this "great country." Seeing the chair helps her "build up courage" and creates almost a euphoric feeling for her. "I'm so lucky, I'm so fortunate, I'm so blessed, my life is so beautiful that I would be able to have this experience, that I live 30 minutes from the Henry Ford and I can come anytime I want." At one point, Mary likens touching the chair to a religious person touching the Pope's robe, a comment she made while describing her reverential reaction to the chair.

Phil had the most explicitly spiritual encounter of all the participants. He called it "earth-shattering," a "revelation," a "religious awakening," the "flame that sparked his heart":

> So I'm standing up there and there's a photograph, there are many of them but one of them that ... as I said, this was like a religious experience to me. This was almost like the clouds opened and like, "Phil, pay attention! You're an Army officer now, you need to grasp the heart and soul of what that really means!" ... I would say there was a good five-minute period there where I was kind of awestruck by all that.

The experience, in fact, changed his life.

Numinous Experiences and The Object Knowledge Framework

In these numinous experiences with objects, there is clear evidence of all of the dimensions of the Object Knowledge Framework. The individual dimension—personal significance—appears to be strongest in these cases, revealing the immediacy of the lived experience as well as the felt qualities of the senses, time, space, and relations with others. There are clear intersections between person and object during the encounters, drawing out prior knowledge, experiences, and opinions. Most of all, there are powerful connections built around each person's identity. But, as the Framework predicts, the dimensions of lifeworld mix with the dimensions of the objectworld. In fact, the numinous study shows how difficult it is to separate these parts of the whole situation. For example, Phil's experience at Little Round Top was powerfully personal, yet it was fused with his understanding of his place in the world, both past and present. The physical presence of the tree (material) made him realize in a profound way his role (individual) as a member of his country and especially as an Army officer (group).

In this study, the theme, Unity of the Moment, is equivalent to what we describe as a *unified experience,* a fusion of the lifeworld and objectworld in a particular moment. This characteristic is actually a thread that runs through the total experience between the person and the object and involves individual, group, and material dimensions all at once. Specifically, the Object Link illustrates our points that an object is incomplete without a person to contemplate it and that the tangible, physical object elicits a more powerful response.

The study on numinous experiences with museum objects demonstrates the concept of a unified experience created through the commingling of the visitor's dimensions and that of the objectworld dimensions. It shows that the visitor also brings something to the museum experience, and museum staff may not know what that is going to be (and that's ok). In fact, this element of surprise—for the visitor as well—defines the unified experience in this case. Surprise means that some aspect of the object is sticking out, is noticeable, and that the object does not simply blend in to the background. Ironically, this surprise is what seems to draw together the whole experience.

Perhaps it is the harmony of the unified experience that best evokes the feelings of reverence in the museum. The commingling of intellect with emotion, the broadening of horizons, and the real, physical thing in one's presence are all essential to this moment. The layers of wonder and majesty—the numinous nature of the experience—help people to make awe-inspiring personal connections with humanity, to people and places we have never known and will never know.

SECTION 3

Object Transformations

Section Three offers strategies for transforming visitor-object experiences through practical examples and exercises for using the Object Knowledge Framework within museum practice. The examples and exercises serve to stimulate new directions for thinking about using objects within museum experiences. In particular we aim to provide both individuals and teams of exhibit developers with the tools to use the Object Knowledge Framework in developing those experiences. Whereas Section Two provided opportunities to see how visitors might experience the world of objects, in Section Three we focus on how museums can transform those objects into more meaningful exchanges. Each chapter includes practical suggestions that focus on elements of design, orientations to exhibition themes, messages, and content as avenues to increase visitor learning. Chapter Six offers strategies for using the Object Knowledge Framework in a project development process and includes exercises and brainstorm suggestions for teams working with object-based experiences. Chapters Seven, Eight, and Nine include activities and examples around the concept of transforming objects through design, content, and participation.

CHAPTER SIX

Using the Object Knowledge Framework

The Object Knowledge Framework underscores the importance of an interdisciplinary and holistic approach to knowing objects and ways to incorporate more personal lived experience into the potential of object-based encounters in the museum. In the next four chapters, we offer a series of strategies and examples for applying the Framework in museum exhibition and program planning. Members of the museum team—from exhibit developer to curator, collections manager to educator, evaluation staff to public relations director—can use the Framework to inform their practice. Employing a visitor-object-centered museum practice does not fall to just one individual staff member, but rather to everyone who thinks about and works on creating meaningful object experiences for visitors. The concept of object knowledge draws on the diverse perspectives of people both inside and outside the museum to help bring the lived experience of objects into the museum.

As we described in earlier chapters, the networked view of museum practice stresses the value of interdisciplinary ways of knowing objects and highlights more opportunities for visitor-object encounters. Networked, or integrated, thinking about visitor-object experiences also draws from a wider array of perspectives on objects which necessarily involves multiple staff perspectives, from that of the curator, the museum educators, the designers, the developers, and so on. This approach provides both staff and visitors opportunities for open exploration rather than narrow, singularly focused interpretations. Museum staff should continue to develop interpretations of objects, just as they always have. But by using a networked approach to thinking about objects and their relationships with people, practitioners can greatly expand their interpretations across a range of disciplines and visitor experiences.

How can this be done? One example is the way museums are now using questions in exhibits to provoke visitor perspectives around an object. Many museums are now encouraging visitors to be equal interpreters of the meaning of the objects they encounter in exhibits. Evans, Mull and Polling (2002) call this process "object-based discourse": objects remain a central component of the visitor experience, but now the museum's presentation of knowledge combines *with* the visitors' perspectives on the meaning of the object. New levels of visitor engagement with objects can be powerful and potentially transformational experiences for both museum staff and visitors alike.

Why would a museum implement the Object Knowledge Framework? Isn't this just the same process museum staff have always followed? Having worked with a wide range of museums, our experience has shown that thinking about the visitor *and* object in a unified experience is not standard practice. For the most part, the traditional method of displaying and interpreting objects continues to focus on the material aspects of an object or on the cultural and social definitions of objects—or on the other end of the spectrum completely, on visitor experience alone. Museums too infrequently attempt to draw out the individualized experiences of the visitor through the object's presence—unless the "personal" orientation is that of the object's initial owner. Very rarely do museums use all three dimensions (individual, group, and material) from either the lifeworld or the objectworld to develop meaningful visitor experiences.

Exercises to Shape Practice

The Object Knowledge Framework advocates for more consistent and integrated inclusion of objects in relation to the goals of a project and encourages more discussion of the potential ways to spark visitor-object encounters that lead to unified experiences. By incorporating its concepts into various steps of exhibition or program planning processes, staff will have more opportunities to create potential moments where visitors can have deeply fulfilling experiences with objects. Imagine the power of the objectworld united with an individual visitor's lifeworld—their individual, group, and material dimensions all bundled up in a cohesive interaction.

But how does a museum enable this? What is the process to support this potentially significant object-based experience for the visitor? Using the Object Knowledge Framework for reflection and intentional planning around concepts and content for exhibitions and programs is one major step in that direction. The Framework might be integrated into team meetings, or it could be the basis for an intensive, focused method for planning. At each of these points, the Framework offers new ways to consider the role of objects in thinking about, planning, and designing experiences for visitors in museum settings. The strategies described here for using the Framework are inherently related to how teams think about and use objects in a project and are customizable to varying circumstances, approaches, and stages of these processes. What follows is a series of exercises that should help museum staff begin to think in the context of the Framework. The exercises are divided into three areas: 1) Exploring different views of the object, 2) Connecting topics and objects, and 3) Transformation of objects into experiences. Because this third area spans a broader perspective on the entire process, we devote Chapters Seven, Eight, and Nine to the strategies for transforming the object into experiences through design, content, and participation.

Along with each of the exercises in this chapter we include several real-life examples based on The Children's Museum of Indianapolis, where Elee Wood serves as scholar-in-residence and where staff helped to test the ideas outlined in this book. In subsequent chapters we provide examples from a wide range of museums from across the United States and England. In the end, the strategies from all three areas can be used one after another in a sequential process, or depending on what the team needs and what time allows, each exercise can be adapted and used separately to suit the specific parameters of each museum's situation.

Exploring Different Views of the Object

WHEN: Early planning.

WHAT: Explore the widest possible range of the lifeworld: views, knowledges, experiences, and understandings surrounding objects.

WHY: To use, but also expand beyond, views about the object held by staff.

Planning always starts with some kind of idea—perhaps a goal for what a visitor might experience or do, or a vision for showcasing a new collection or specific object. Whatever its origin, exhibit teams can apply the Object Knowledge Framework to develop their thinking about the role of objects in every aspect of the project. This might involve deciding how to communicate the meaning and purpose of an object, or how to integrate objects into an existing theme. The Framework examines the lifeworld of the person and the objectworld through the individual, group, and material dimensions. Reflecting on prior experiences that staff have had with the objects related to the exhibition or program concepts can help generate and refine ideas for a project.

In order to explore a variety of different views of objects, museum staff must be aware of their own knowledge and expertise, recognizing that it may be different from that of most visitors—and possibly from other staff members. To be successful in transforming a general project idea into visitor experiences with objects, the team must, from the very beginning, monitor their collective personal knowledge, expertise, history, memory, and connections to the objects. It is unavoidable that personal connections will influence the interpretation, explanation, or description of the objects. But taking time early on in the development and idea generation process to reflect on—and then expand beyond—personal understandings of an object allows for more stories to come to the surface and may result in an expanded range of visitor experiences. This openness affords greater depth of knowledge for team members and can reveal more options for communicating and transforming the big idea or concept for the visitor.

This process acknowledges that *every* person, staff and visitor alike, participating in the project has connections to the objects. Visitors come to the museum with their own range of knowledge, interests, and affiliations with objects. They pay attention to things they are interested in and have a wide range of responses. Hooper-Greenhill (2000) explains these ways of looking at objects as functions of an "interpretive community." Visitors and museum staff all belong to different interpretive communities, whether they know it or not. Each of these "communities" uses different strategies and background knowledge for looking at objects. This means that it is incredibly important to know how, early on, the museum staff regard the selected objects and the extent that this will influence the exhibition or project: "If exhibitions speak only to the interpretive community to which the curator belongs, unless visitors share these interpretive frameworks, they will not feel comfortable" (Hooper-Greenhill, 2000, p. 123).

Drawing on the contributions of multiple interpretive communities will strengthen the team's ability to spark greater interest for visitors. It may also create new avenues for exploration by the team members. In short, the more ways that the team can look at the objects, the more opportunity there is to bring new light to the project. In this section, we offer three exercises that draw out these multiple understandings and hidden meanings.

EXERCISE 1. *Personal Object Reflections*

Museum staff can use this exercise to elicit their current knowledge around the objects they plan to include in an exhibition or program project. In this activity, each staff member writes his or her responses to a series of questions and shares them with the group. By organizing and analyzing this information, the team can get a sharper picture of their own preferences for looking at the objects. Thinking about their individual relationships with objects helps everyone on the team gain perspective on where interpretations of objects can influence the planning process. When contemplating the different schemes each member of the team uses to make sense of the topic or objects, it is useful to ask a series of questions that are based on the exhibition objects, content, and/or big idea.

- What do you know about this object? Write freely about everything that comes to mind: How would you define it? Where did it come from? What does it mean?
- Do you have a concrete memory that this object conjures up for you? What is it? Who was there? What happened?
- Have you had an experience with the object? What was it about? Who was there? What did you do? How did you feel?

FOLLOW UP. After team members complete their responses, gather all of the information to search for various patterns or themes that emerge. This could be done by having staff look at the compiled responses and determining common themes, or generating a "word cloud" where the frequencies of words are represented by font size (e.g. the larger the font size means the more words represented in the sample).

WHAT DOES IT LOOK LIKE? ***Personal Object Reflections: Star Toy.*** *Star Toys* involved a very straightforward display of approximately 25 different toys and figures from a variety of space-themed movies and television programs, as well as models of different space travel vehicles available between the 1950s and early 2000s (Figure 6.1). The big idea for the exhibit was to show how real life space travel and science fiction storytelling influenced and inspired each other. Students working with the curators tested out the personal interpretation questions by reflecting on some of the objects included in the exhibit. Table 6.1 shows five different team member's responses to one object included in the exhibit: a model of the Starship Enterprise, from *Star Trek*, ca. 1994.

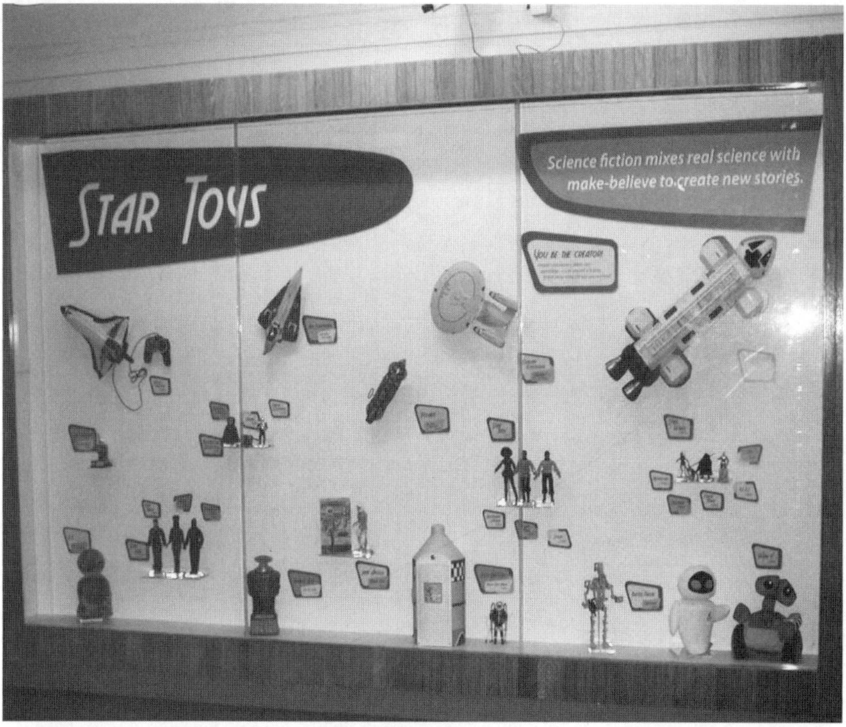

FIGURE 6.1 Star Toys Case. Photo © The Children's Museum of Indianapolis.

TABLE 6.1 Team Responses on Objects

Team Member	***To the best of your ability, define what you know about the Starship Enterprise, Star Trek, ca. 1994?***	***Where possible give a personal experience you had with the object?***
1	This is the main space ship in the television show that is commanded by Captain James Luck Piccard [sic]. This is not [from] the original series from the 1970s.	Watched this show occasionally when growing up. Started my appreciation of Patrick Stewart's acting.
2	I think this is the ship from Star Trek. I am by no means a 'Trekkie' but watched the original series as well as the Next Generation.	Just watching the show with my old roommate
3	Star Trek members lived on it, travels through space, has a portal on it, scientifically advanced.	My mom watched it, I occasionally watched it, represented down time for my mom.

(continued on the following page)

TABLE 6.1 Team Responses on Objects *(continued)*

Team Member	*To the best of your ability, define what you know about the Starship Enterprise, Star Trek, ca. 1994?*	*Where possible give a personal experience you had with the object?*
4	This is a grey plastic toy replica of the spaceship used in the TV series and movies.	I never played with any Star Trek toys, and I never watched the TV show, but I do remember going with my dad to see one of the Star Trek movies. I didn't get a lot of one-on-one time with my dad so I enjoyed seeing it with him.
5	Has had five models, A-C on the original Trek and in the movies, D on Next Gen, and E in the Next Gen crew movies. Flagship of the Federation.	Loved the show and what it represents as a kind of ambassador ship for humanity. Made me a fan of all things Star Trek.

These five examples show the different kinds of information that each person has about the *Star Trek* Enterprise object. The first three responses represent casual viewers of the television program. Through them, each team member demonstrates some knowledge of the show's premise, recognizes the broader cultural connections, and describes the characters and the object in question. In providing a definition of the object, the second member indicates a very clear distinction between the type of knowledge that a "Trekkie" would have and how that influences what she does and does not know about the object. The fourth team member's description focuses primarily on the material qualities of the model. The fifth team member offers a highly detailed description, including the relationship of various models of the ship and the specific features of the ship within the television program. Each of these personal responses to an object in the exhibit reflects a distinct and very specific instance or time when the person was connected to the *Star Trek* television program. Note especially, that even the fourth member, despite her lack of knowledge of the television show, has a personal link that relates a unique bond with her father when seeing the object.

In the preceding examples, each person described the object using a variety of interpretive communities—fans of the show ("Trekkies") and consumers of popular culture (occasional viewer, important to others). This knowledge comes from their personal experience of the television program rather than from the object itself.

EXERCISE 2. *Public Perceptions Investigation*

What are the most common public perceptions of this object to date? This activity follows the personal reflection on the objects, and requires the team to investigate how the object might look to the visitor or outside world. It involves research in current popular conceptions of objects like the ones they are considering. The exercise helps the team learn more about the ways that visitors from different audience segments might view an object as well as the extent of public knowledge on a particular topic. Here are a few ways to do this:

- Gather examples of the object in literature and media. Pay attention to user-generated content from sources like Facebook, Flickr, Twitter, Wikipedia or Pinterest.
- Generate examples and sources from scholarship on the topic or about the object.
- Investigate interest-specific groups that have deep knowledge and expertise about the topic. Collect information on how the group describes, explains, or thinks about the object. This could be gathered through listservs, clubs, or organizational websites.
- Develop a front-end evaluation strategy that asks your visitors what they know. Consider conducting "object interviews" with visitors around prospective objects that might be included in the exhibit.

During this process, the team should review the information gathered for patterns or themes. The team can compare these themes with those generated from their own individual experiences (see Exercise 1). For example, during very early planning for an exhibition on the Chinese Terracotta Warriors at The Children's Museum of Indianapolis, team members searched the World Wide Web for the most commonly used images and top ten family-oriented websites related to the topic. Then, they generated word maps based on the content from these websites to gain insight on frequently used terms and concepts.

WHAT DOES IT LOOK LIKE? ***Public Perceptions Investigation: Object interviews at the Children's Museum of Indianapolis*** Staff at The Children's Museum of Indianapolis needed to think carefully about how to help visitors make sense of an extremely rare and unusual type of fossil: a fossil of a mummified dinosaur. To better understand visitor perceptions on the differences between mummified remains and fossilized remains, they developed a set of front-end evaluation strategies to find out more about the public perception and knowledge. They first met with visitors in a focus group and then conducted a series of object interviews with museum visitors in the galleries.

During the focus group, family members got a chance to see the fossil of a mummified dinosaur that would be in the exhibit. Questions for the focus group emphasized looking and thinking about the fossil. The exhibit developer and curator asked the families to start with one-word descriptions about what they saw and any guesses on what the object might be. They also asked why the families answered the way they did. Throughout the focus group, the exhibit developer focused on the kinds of questions that families asked, the kinds of things they were curious about, and how their questions changed as they learned more about the fossil. The object interviews followed a similar line of questioning. These interviews consisted of short, 10-minute sessions led by the exhibit developer and gallery interpretation staff. Visitors could look at and talk about an object and images related to mummified fossils; the staff then asked visitors to describe what they saw and the kinds of questions they had about the things they saw.

The results from the focus groups and object interviews indicated that many visitors have very specific ideas about what makes a mummy and what makes a fossil, but they are confused about the idea of a fossil that came from a mummified dinosaur. The goal of the exhibit is to explain the significance of this new discovery and introduce the significance of these kinds of fossils to the audience. With these front-end evaluation findings, the team now has a more developed understanding of visitor knowledge and will be able to use a variety of objects in addition to the fossil to develop the content.

EXERCISE 3. *Group Knowledge of Objects in Shaping Meaning*

Following the reflection of personal object understandings (Exercise 1), and then the collection of public perceptions and knowledge about selected objects (Exercise 2), the team can conduct an assessment of the objects and how they shape meaning across different interest groups. A series of questions like those that follow structures this process. The team can use these questions as part of background research, or the highlight of a planning session where the team generates answers with advisory groups or focus groups on charts or a whiteboard. The questions can also enhance the extent of the team's knowledge about this dimension of the Object Knowledge Framework or challenge the team to think in new directions. The following questions are a general guide for working with the group dimension:

- How does the group "frame" or situate the object? What unspoken ideas or kinds of information are made visible or revealed through these "frames"?
- What are the different perspectives that the group has on the object, and how do these relate to the information and knowledge of the intended audiences?
- How are knowledge and power connected to the object?
- How does the object shape group or social identity?
- What does the group already know about the object? What past interpretations or understandings might still be in play?

The process of sorting through this information, both as individual staff and as team members, reveals the multiple meanings and representations of objects that are possible within the project.

WHAT DOES IT LOOK LIKE? ***Group Knowledge of Objects: The Power of Children.*** Going deeper into a process of examining objects takes time, but the results provide much greater insight into the meaning and role of objects in exhibitions. Taking the time to look closely at what the object reveals across the different dimensions of the Object Knowledge Framework affords broader access to messages in an exhibit setting. The following example comes from front-end testing of ideas with youth focus groups for *The Power of Children: Making a Difference* at The Children's Museum of Indianapolis. These responses provide a thought-provoking view on the group dimensions of the Framework. Members of the exhibit team asked a group of seventh graders completing a unit of study on Anne Frank to share their views on Anne Frank's diary and its significance in telling her story.

Seeing the diary was clearly a main draw for students. When describing the experience of reading the diary, the students' lived experience came through clearly: "Her diary feels real when you read it and it tells exactly how the Jews felt during WWII. The diary makes you think about how horrible the Nazis were and makes you not want anything like the Holocaust to happen again." They also saw parallels as teenagers: "She was a kid at the age that my friends and I are now, yet she had so many thoughts and dreams. Most people don't write about things like that in a diary, and if they do, what they write about doesn't usually have any content of significance. Hers did." When the exhibit developers asked the youth focus groups how they would want to interact with the diary and Anne Frank's story, they wanted to be able to be a part of it in some way. Their interest in being able to make their mark on the diary may be a way to demonstrate empathy and connection to Anne and the story. Many of them indicated an interest in being able to physically interact with the book in some way, as a way to connect with Anne and her story.

Connecting Topics and Objects

WHEN: During development, planning and design stages.

WHAT: Identify ways to connect the objectworld with the project big idea, goals, or messages.

WHY: To develop strong connections between exhibition content, visistor experiences, and objects.

The second major area for using the Object Knowledge Framework is the process of connecting topics and objects. In this process, team members further develop their conceptions of the objectworld within the overarching project topic. This is a point in the process where linking concepts and messages of the exhibition with objects becomes very important. It requires the team to look at how objects convey key information or messages for the project. Similarly, the team can use this strategy for an in-depth investigation of the objectworld and how that may be reflected to visitors.

Having a "big idea" (Serrell, 1996) and/or key takeaway messages for an experience is critical to the exhibit development process. What this phase tends to lack, especially around the topic of objects in the museum experience, is careful thinking about the relationship between potential big ideas and the objects that might be included in the project—and perhaps more importantly, how these can ultimately support rich visitor experiences. As described earlier, the disciplinary and content knowledge of staff members often drives the overall interpretation of the big idea. It is not uncommon to make the object selections before developing the big idea or theme of a project (as in an object driven exhibition), or well after determining the big idea (as in a theme driven exhibition). But taking the time to be intentional about object selections can better support the development of the unified visitor-object experience in relation to the big idea for the project.

In this section, we present two different brainstorming exercises that give the project team new perspectives on chosen objects. The first exercise focuses on the objects that relate to the project big idea; the second exercise looks at the object's point of view in relation to the big idea.

EXERCISE 4. *Big-Idea-to-Object Brainstorming*

This exercise further refines the project's big idea and its relationship with objects in the exhibition. The goal for this brainstorming process is to plot out prospective objects that represent those concepts important to the project. Objects play a large part in communicating the project's messages and content, and serve as representations of those ideas; they are a concrete demonstration of what the team wants to portray.

STEP 1 The team brainstorms all of the possible objects that could be related to the project big idea and its related messages. The goal is to think expansively; the list of possible objects should not necessarily be limited to the museum's collection. This can be done on a white board, on individual note cards, or sticky notes.

STEP 2 Then, the group reviews the objects and puts them into groups. The objects can be grouped together in many different ways, or organized in relation to the components of the project concepts. The team can play around with different groupings.

STEP 3 The team organizes the categories and groupings according to the project's messages and content, and how well they represent those ideas. Identify which categories are most important, which are worth knowing, and which are merely useful but not essential.

STEP 4 Now, consider the relationship of the objects and themes to the big idea.

FOLLOW UP. The team can ask themselves a series of questions about the groupings:

- Does this grouping adequately illustrate our point? Does it strongly illustrate our point?
- Did we "settle" for any objects in our group?
- Did our message(s) match our objects?
- Would the message be the same without the object present?
- What would the exhibit look like with only the objects present (no interpretation)?
- Did objects organize smoothly into our groupings or did we have to "make them fit"?

- Did a new grouping/message emerge from the brainstorm of possible objects?
- What are we missing?

WHAT DOES IT LOOK LIKE? ***Big-Idea-to-Object Brainstorming: Terra Cotta Warriors.*** Team members used the Big-Idea-to-Object process in a brainstorm session for the exhibition on Chinese Terracotta Warriors at The Children's Museum of Indianapolis. The main theme for brainstorming was "Painted Terracotta Warriors," The goal was to generate as many different objects related to this idea as possible, with a focus on art and science. Here is the list of objects they developed:

head pieces	weapons	lacquer	casts
tools	dig pits	textiles	brushes
tiles	pigments	tools	paint
horses	chemicals	clay	
actual warriors	paint chips	lapis	
tomb	minerals	molds	

Once the team had generated the list, they organized the objects and ideas into different categories related to the exhibition plan—site discovery, site excavation, conservation, and warrior construction. The groups then discussed the role of the objects in relation to these larger themes for the exhibition using the Seeing-the-Objectworld exercise in the next section. The discussion that followed from this exercise reinforced for the team the importance of finding objects that illustrated a story, rather than simply highlighting the objects themselves. The team focused on the ways that the messages could be delivered with the objects they selected, as well as what objects were missing from the narrative they wanted to tell. This process also stimulated ideas on how the objects could be used to demonstrate exhibit messages as well as provide a context for interactive experiences.

EXERCISE 5. *Seeing the Objectworld*

The next exercise helps the team think carefully about the dimensions of the objectworld and all the ways that objects on the list generated in Exercise 4 can represent, transform, or even mediate the meaning of the big idea. This strategy is about objects *transforming* the project concepts, rather than simply representing them. A second brainstorming session now explores the big idea—by looking at the objectworld in the context of the big idea. The goal is to reflect carefully on all the possible ways the team can understand a specific object or its function in the context of the big idea.

This exercise can be done individually (as members of the team) or as part of a team-based discussion, either as a worksheet or in a brainstorm/discussion format. For each specific object or set of related objects, answer the following questions along all of the Object Knowledge Framework dimensions. The goal is to arrive at integrated ways that the dimensions of the objectworld support the big idea, and establish areas where more research might be necessary.

QUESTIONS TO HIGHLIGHT THE INDIVIDUAL DIMENSION

- How does the object mobilize emotions, perceptions, or values?
- How does the object influence the way people feel and think?
- How does the object shape personal identity?
- What's the object's story? Where did it come from?
- What is the object's connection to an individual (within the context of the big idea)?
- How does the object relate to or reflect various individual experiences in connection to the big idea?
- What has it done in the past? To whom did it belong?
- What is the possible relationship between the object and a visitor in connection to the big idea?

QUESTIONS TO HIGHLIGHT THE GROUP DIMENSION

- What is the object's connection to different cultural groups, societies, or ways of knowing (in the context of the big idea)?
- How does the object connect to humans over time?
- How does the object connect to humans through space or place?
- How does the object affect larger shared issues of society/humanity/group?
- What events or happenings does the object "see" in the specific place and time of the big idea?
- When or how does the object play a role in these events?

QUESTIONS TO HIGHLIGHT THE MATERIAL DIMENSION

- How was the object used? How was it made? Who made it and why? How is it used at present?
- How many lives has it had? Has it been used for different things over time?
- How can the material quality of the object evoke a response from visitors? How does it feel? What is the texture? How heavy is it? What does it sound like? What does it smell like?
- What material aspects of the object tell a story that might be different from other interpretations?

Based on these responses, the team can now begin to formulate ways that different objects might help visitors make more sense of the big idea. Going through this process can lead to identification of powerful images and emotional connections to objects. For example, in a well-known section of the permanent exhibition at The United States Holocaust Memorial Museum, visitors enter a single, stark room that is full of hundreds of shoes of all shapes and sizes confiscated from prisoners in one of the death camps. On the wall a piece of poetry tells the story of the shoes—from their perspective as witnesses to the destruction of their owners. This use of thousands of shoes serves as a vivid and intense demonstration of objects to communicate an important message. The poetry combined with an over-powering smell and the visual image of the shoes constructs a simple, yet extremely evocative point of view. The significance of these objects and their placement helps to give visitors perspective and creates a powerful emotional experience.

FOLLOW UP. Compared to the Big-Idea-to-Object brainstorming exercises described earlier, the process used in Seeing the Objectworld gives more direction to the selection and identification of objects and/or collections items that reflect or demonstrate the big idea and can lead toward visitor-object encounters. Thinking carefully through this process, teams can begin to define and develop criteria for the kind of objects that could be included in the experience. Recognizing the wide range of meaning that each object takes on can help develop a more dynamic and evocative orientation to the subject matter. Furthermore, this process will open new avenues for design discussions, strategies for further developing the content areas, and opportunities for visitor participation in experiences and programs.

WHAT DOES IT LOOK LIKE? *Seeing the Objectworld: The Emperor's Painted Army.* After completing the Big-Idea-to-Object Brainstorming, Children's Museum Terracotta Warriors team members then used Seeing-the-Objectworld questions. The team divided themselves into smaller groups related to the major thematic areas intended for the exhibition and used the questions from the material, group, and individual dimensions. Because the project was still at the conceptual phase, the team used these questions to develop their big idea. Table 6.2 on the following page shows example responses for two of the proposed objects within the exhibition—the warrior figures and paint fragments.

At this point, the team began to generate statements related to the ideas generated from Seeing the Objectworld. Each group tried to distill their ideas into a series of statements that might shape the message of each area of the exhibition. Then, they clustered these statements into major themes to generate an overarching concept for the big idea. As a result of these brainstorming sessions, the team began to refine and focus the concepts to more fully relate to the different ways the objects might be used in the exhibition.

Transforming Objects into Experiences

WHEN: Development, design, and implementation

WHAT: Moving from conceptual planning to fully realized exhibit elements and experiences

WHY: Provide more meaningful connections for visitors in the exhibition

The third area for using the Object Knowledge Framework moves beyond the conceptual phases of planning and transforms object experiences within the overall project. Instead of a series of exercises, we offer a set of maxims—ways to think about how museum work is done and how it affects the end results. Those moments where museum visitors might have a unified experience with an object stem from a wide range of individual connections that museum staff cannot control. But what the museum staff *does* have the power to create in exhibitions and programs are situations where those moments are most likely to emerge. Transforming or translating the objectworld into something accessible to visitors means museum staff can work intentionally, through a variety of strategies, to build situations and environments that encourage unified experiences (Figure 6.2). This is the exciting proposition of museum work: creating transformative settings and

Table 6.2 Seeing the Objectworld: Terracotta Warriors and Paint Fragments

Question	The Warriors	Paint Fragments
How does the object relate to or reflect various individual experiences in connection to the big idea?	The skill of the Chinese artists captured the individuality and emotion that we can relate to today. Some visitors will be artists, soldiers, interested in fashion (hair/beards/costume), weapons, China.	Lots of people have or purchase decorative painted objects. They may be familiar with the ideas of decoration and how that changes over time.
What is the object's possible relationship to a visitor in connection to the big idea?	How can I step into the shoes of a warrior? What would it be like to create a warrior?	How can I tell the difference between the real thing and a recreation? What can I learn from this to help me fix things of my own?
What are the object's connections to humans over time?	The clay warriors represent a relationship with actual warriors as a substitute for burial with the Emperor. It closes the gap of time because we can recreate the warriors as people we can still recognize.	Created and applied by people. Thousands of years later it is studied and conserved. Paint is something everyone can relate to in some way. We can see it fade over time in our own lives.
What events or happenings does the object "see" in the specific place and time of the big idea?	Was the full complex of warriors ever seen in its own time? The politics of then and now also gives some perspective on the role of Emperor Qin's goal. The contrast between the hidden aspect of the Warrior's origin and the fact that now they are being seen by thousands of people is important.	As objects are revealed in contemporary conditions the paint fades and flakes off almost immediately. Conservators are trying to figure out how to protect and preserve the paint. They are also looking for patterns and processes for how the paint was created and applied.

opportunities for the visitor's lifeworld and the objectworld to intersect. Decisions at this level can make a big difference in how the visitor will experience an exhibition or program. In museums, the transformation of objects happens through:

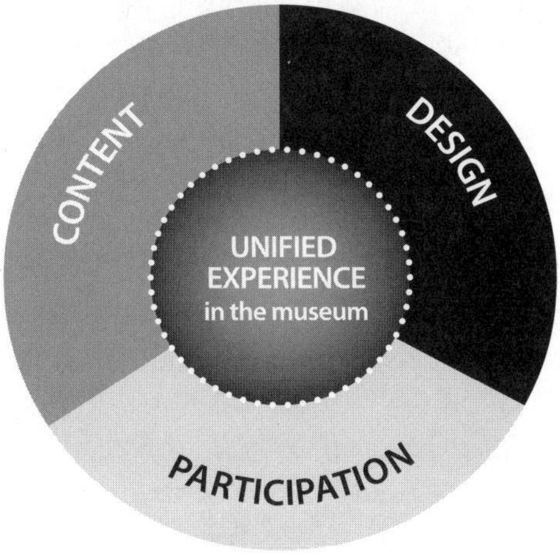

FIGURE 6.2 Transformation of Objects.

- **Design:** how the project shows or reveals the topic;
- **Content:** how the object connects to the topic; and
- **Participation:** what visitors can do with the topic.

In the next section, we briefly define each of the three paths to transformation and then introduce a set of maxims to help guide these transformations before moving on to the next three chapters where we go into greater depth on all three.

Design

The primary focus of design thinking is about how visual cues and information show the visitor what the team wants them to know, think about, or do. Design is everywhere in our environment. Elements of design aid the generation of a wide range of emotional outcomes and directed attention. Think of design as a strategic approach to help visitors achieve a unique expectation. Through careful, clever, and conscious design, teams can say a lot using objects and sometimes, little else.

Content

As teams develop ideas for a project they need to pay attention to content and how much information the use of objects as a form of content adds to or enhances a visitor's knowledge and experience. Think intently about what the object represents in terms of content, potential content, or unintended reactions. Make note of the object relationship to ideas based on its placement in a case, the exhibit, or even the museum as a whole. This can be challenging—especially depending on the age of the audience, the local context, or even in the complexity of the content itself.

Participation

The participatory approaches for unified visitor-object experience are the educational strategies linked to the project and beyond. As with the design and content, there should be some deliberation on what the visitor is expected to do, know, or think about after visiting the exhibition or program. However, what the visitor takes away from the experience should not be confused with their open-ended exploration of ideas. Instead, the team can look at how engaging with the object through different activities such as hands-on exploration, questioning strategies, or live interpretation further communicates the goals for the project. Letting visitors choose what they want to see or do, and having some kind structure in a museum experience are both necessary elements in helping the visitor feel successful and motivated to participate or even just to stick with an experience.

Maxims to Guide Transformation

We have developed a set of "maxims" intended to serve as easily remembered ideas that support unified visitor-object experiences in all three areas of transformation—design, content, and participation. Of course, these three areas are not totally distinct in practice.

These maxims provide guidance for museum staff to transform ideas about objects into an exhibition or program intentionally and purposefully while, at the same time, keeping an open mind on how the overall visitor experience will play out. This means being open to the unexpected and the unending possibilities that visitors bring. Knowing that the visitor is part of the equation in the development of a "unified experience" means that museum staff are not fully in control once the exhibition or program is underway. What *is* under the control of staff is the capacity to think carefully about the way that visitors might connect to personal experiences, the shared group and cultural experiences that might come with an object, and the object's materiality. Museum staff have control over designing the environment—through lighting, visual appeal, colors, placement of objects, pathways, etc. They also have control over the physical and metaphorical placement of the object in relation to the big idea. In the end, the visitor is the one who will have an experience, and museum professionals must be thoughtful about creating conditions that will make that experience meaningful and memorable—one that ideally leads to a unified visitor-object experience.

THE 12 MAXIMS FOR OBJECT TRANSFORMATION

Design	1.	Do cool things.
	2.	Break the rules.
	3.	Be up front.
	4.	Don't forget simplicity and balance.
Content	5.	An object is worth 1000 meanings.
	6.	Make it personal.
	7.	Leave room for more.
	8.	It's all connected.
Participation	9.	The physical matters.
	10.	Help people reach greater heights.
	11.	Make it come alive.
	12.	Start with end in mind.

All twelve maxims contribute to building a strong connection between object and visitor. The design maxims speak to purposeful thinking about using objects in museums. The content maxims address the complex relationship between content and meanings. The participation maxims put the visitor-object encounter in the center of the experience. There will always be variation in the type of encounters visitors have with objects: some will be purely informative and others will be transformational and deeply moving. The visitor ultimately holds the capacity to have a unified experience. Most importantly, focusing on these maxims will help museum staff work toward building experiences that have the potential to make a deep impact in the lives of each individual visitor. Because the area of transformation spans the entire process of the museum, the following three chapters are devoted to design, content, and participation, explaining each maxim and providing exercises and examples for each that are intended to expand the use of the Object Knowledge Framework.

CHAPTER SEVEN

Transformation through Design

In Chapter Six we provided a broad overview of the Object Knowledge Framework and introduced the three areas through which to integrate the planning and development of visitor-object experiences. Because the concept of transformation as used here is expansive, we organized our discussion by design, content, and participation, each its own chapter. Within each chapter we outline the corresponding maxims, or guiding principles, which we introduced at the end of Chapter Six. The maxims for the transformation of object experiences can provide museum staff ways to re-think the use and value of objects through design, content, and participation. As in the previous chapter, we continue with a series of exercises and questions for contemplation for each of the transformations, followed by real-life illustrations from a range of museums across the United States and England.

Thinking about Design

Transformation of objects through design starts with the question, "How do I show, or reveal to people, the objectworld in different contexts?" Design is not simply about the aesthetics of an exhibit—although that certainly has much to do with it. Rather, design is about change and is focused first and foremost on human behavior and quality of experience. It is an activity that translates an idea into a blueprint for something useful: a car, a building, a graphic, a service, or a process. The most important element of design is that the designer is *translating* an idea into another format. Design encompasses a wide range of processes that incorporate intuition, imagination, ideas, ideals, empathy, and of course, style (Neumeier, 2009). At a more practical level, design also incorporates sound, light, texture, smell, movement, and so forth.

Elizabeth Wood and Kiersten F. Latham, "Transformation through Design" in *The Objects of Experience: Transforming Visitor-Object Encounters in Museums*, pp 118-131.

In museum work, everyone is a designer in some form or another. Clearly, exhibition designers have an eye toward visual elements—the look and feel of an experience, its flow. The staff that transform objects through design must also draw on creative thinking, innovation, and problem-solving. Through these aspects of design, the overall team goal is to evoke a response from the visitors. How do we use design to create a moment where a visitor can have the powerful, unified experience with an object? In the following discussion, the first four design-related maxims are accompanied by real life examples, demonstrating these principles in action as well as ideas on how to put them into practice.

MAXIM 1. **Do cool things.**

If you were a visitor, what would you want to see or do? What generates intrigue or interest? What makes people curious? What draws people in? How do you create an evocative moment?

Because everyone has different definitions of "cool," this first maxim really forces teams to think expansively about constructing evocative experiences. An evocative experience connects a person to deeper emotions; it is the moment where people express "oohs" and "ahas," or even "whoas." These instinctive reactions suggest potentials for delight or awe, or sometimes surprise. Keeping in mind that the unity of the person and object comes from making connections to individual, group, and material experiences, the way the object is displayed is crucial. Doing cool things is about doing something unexpected with an object; it incorporates strong images that lead to memories and feelings. Doing cool things is not about gimmickry or novelty; it is about showing ideas in unexpected ways that bring the ideas and objects in a museum experience to life.

Think for a second about an exhibit or program experience that took your breath away. What was going on? How did it evoke that kind of response? That's the way cool things work. Here are some things you can do to "do cool things," followed by examples of a few "cool things" in exhibitions and program experiences with objects.

EXERCISE 6. *Look Book Reflection*

Creating cool things means keeping an eye out for what evokes an emotional response in you and others. People collect ideas and examples of things they think are cool in many different ways. One strategy for thinking further on this idea is to start keeping track of things that are "cool," interesting, and evocative. Take pictures and create a "look book" or scrapbook of ideas that work together. Computer and Web-based applications can help organize and sort ideas, images and references. Sitting down with ideas, and looking carefully and reflecting on their composition, can help you find the secret behind what makes things "cool." For each of the ideas and visuals in the look book or in a project, explain what makes them cool or interesting. Ask yourself: What is going in this situation on that evokes the kind of emotional or inspired response? When this is complete, create a word cloud or other visual reminder to keep on file.

EXERCISE 7. *Messing Around with Objects*

Take some time with an object to look carefully at its features. Ask the following questions:

- What would make a visitor interested in looking just a bit longer?
- What could catch the visitor's eye?
- What could draw attention to the object in such a way that it reveals beauty, connection, or caring?
- How can the positioning of the object create a message?
  - How can you exaggerate the object?
  - How can you rearrange the object?
  - How do you position the object less seriously?
  - In what ways might contrasting visual elements help to evoke a mood? Think about pairings like light with dark, large with small, rough with smooth, natural with manufactured.

WHAT DOES MAXIM 1 LOOK LIKE? **Making Art with Fish: *Open Sea,* Monterey Bay Aquarium, Monterey, California.** Most people don't expect to walk into an aquarium and have an emotional response to fish. However, at Monterey Bay Aquarium, that's exactly the goal. The exhibits at the aquarium are an immersive experience into the world of creatures that live in and near the sea. For many people there's something very exciting about the way these exhibits evoke feelings and connections to the animals. Nearly every exhibit element highlights some aspect of the animal's habitat or biology through case design, lighting, and text. To achieve this, the teams at the Aquarium take a particular approach to their project planning and design that emphasizes beauty, making connections to people, and an ethos of caring. These qualities are deeply connected to the museum's mission and vision.

One of the most breathtaking of the exhibits is *Open Sea*. The exhibition begins with a shimmering, glittering school of live sardines swimming in a large circular tank overhead. A singular line of poetry appears to float on the walls of the entryway. You can hear people gasp as they enter in awe. On entering, a child exclaimed, "It almost looks real!"—perhaps a testament to the surreal feeling she had. Further along visitors encounter an array of live jellyfish floating freely in dramatically lit tanks that make the fish glow with almost unearthly vibrancy. Beyond, a huge 90-foot expanse of glass reveals the placid life of the underwater world. Visitors can stand face to face with schools of fish and watch as turtles, rays, and other creatures swim in the enormous tank.

What is striking about the way *Open Sea* delivers its message is the care and focus on making the features of the animals stand out. By drawing on the enormity of the ocean, the tightly packed movements of certain schools of fish, and the ethereal qualities of jellyfish illuminated by special lighting, the designers have created the unexpected; that is what makes this exhibit so evocative. The Aquarium staff operate from a set of the principles around making things beautiful, building personal connections, and engendering a sense of caring, which help to drive the emotional and aesthetic qualities they value. These operating principles all contribute to what makes a very "cool" exhibit.

WHAT DOES MAXIM 1 LOOK LIKE? **Bringing Pictures to Life: *Maker's Mark Distillery Tour*, Loretto, Kentucky.** Whether you drink bourbon or not, the red wax seal of a Maker's Mark bottle is a fairly notable trademark. What's also interesting is how the staff at Maker's Mark chose to tell their story to distillery visitors. From the moment one arrives in the rolling hills of the property, the idea of *family* is prominent. Visitors begin their tour in the welcome center, which is carefully built and decorated to suggest the large family home of distillery founder T. William Samuels, Sr. The entryway leads to a living room with sofas and chairs, and a large fireplace and mantle covered with family photos. An adjacent dining room has several framed photos of the Samuels family along with a series of notebooks that show early designs for the Maker's Mark logo. In the kitchen, a tall urn of real lemonade is available for sipping. As well, there are further telltale signs of the distinctive Maker's Mark trademark: a coffee urn dripping with red wax sits in the corner, suggesting the idea that someone has been experimenting. Further on in the family library, a telephone sits on a table along with a few other notebooks and sketches, as well as a number of books.

At first glance some of the notable elements like the design books and coffee urn indicate a connection to the company's branding. But if a visitor lingers a bit longer in certain rooms, something really "cool" happens. In the dining room, each of the framed photos very slowly comes to life. For just a second a visitor might catch the movement—a cough, a yawn, a raised eyebrow. These are timed so that not everyone will see the movement, often leaving people to think their eyes are playing tricks on them. Suddenly, the photos come to life and begin a dialogue. Each family member contributes to telling the story of how the bourbon recipe came to be. In the family library, the telephone will ring on occasion. The visitor who is curious (or brave) enough to pick up the phone is rewarded with a humorous account of family members sneaking off for a dip in the pond and other "secrets" about the family business. These features create unexpected moments of delight and generate the feeling of family connections that help to create anticipation and excitement about the upcoming tour.

MAXIM 2. **Break rules.**

What rule can you break in order to open up possibilities for the viewer? What unintended consequences might occur? How do you need to accommodate these potential effects?

In Section One we discussed the need to break out of disciplinary silos. These divisions can limit the options for building exhibitions and programs that promote visitor-object encounters. In some cases, the division of content-specific knowledge or approaches to describing objects creates dissonance for museum visitors. The everyday world is not always divided into neat geographical or chronological patterns, categories of artistic media, or even convenient clusters of exemplary works. More frequently, people experience the everyday world as a mix of thematic ideas, time periods, places, and messages. The divide between expert knowledge and the everyday experiences of museum visitors can therefore mean the difference between an engaged visitor and someone who feels alienated because they perceive a lack of their own expertise.

The rules and expectations of what *should* be on display or what *ought* to be part of a museum exhibition might be the very things that prevent museum staff from moving from traditional, hierarchical practices to new integrated, networked practices. In this case the "rules" that teams can break are usually the unwritten rules that come from disciplinary process, habits, and various assumptions about the way things are (or should be) done. Being able to discern rules that can be broken and rules that actually support success is the first step in learning how to challenge them. Think for a moment about the different "rules" that come with museum practices—Do paintings really need to be hung at eye level? (And really... *whose* eye level?) Does every object need a label? Who says the ceiling and floor are off limits?

Just as doing cool things is about capturing the visitor's attention, the idea of breaking the rules can do the same thing. This kind of transformation through a design strategy happens in a number of ways—whether changing themes, intentionally working across disciplines, or even displaying something backwards, sideways, upside down, or inside out.

In order to break rules, one has to know some basics. Just as jazz improvisation draws on deep knowledge of chord progressions, knowing how things fit together helps people get a better sense of what assumptions or expectations are driving the decision making. The following exercises can help staff investigate some of these often hidden, invisible structures.

EXERCISE 8. *Questions for Rule Breaking*

Think about your project. Consider the following questions:

- What unusual or unexpected ideas can spur your thinking in a new direction? (Go ahead and share that wacky idea!)
- Which rules can you break? Which rules can't you break? What even *are* the rules?
- Think of five ways you did something in the last two exhibits/programs your museum created and list an alternative way of doing each.
- What isn't said in the exhibition? Why?
- What unusual combinations can you create?
- How can you emphasize different elements of an object? What one area can be different?
- What if the object was isolated? How can you make it stand out?
- What would look like backwards? Upside-down?
- What if you used ten of the same object to make your point? Fifty? A thousand?
- How does the location of the object help to emphasize (or deemphasize) its importance?

WHAT DOES MAXIM 2 LOOK LIKE? A Modern Cabinet of Curiosity: *Connecting Cultures*, Brooklyn Museum, Brooklyn, New York. Walking into the *Connecting Cultures* exhibition at the Brooklyn Museum is like walking into a modern cabinet of curiosity, the early Renaissance version of museums packed with objects of all sorts. Images and objects fill the room from the floor to the very tall ceilings: they are positioned in compartmentalized wall units, hung at every level, and mounted in a variety of cases and on pedestals. As visitors enter the space, the gallery introduction provides background on the traditional organization of museum objects—chronologically, geographically, or by medium. In this gallery space however, the museum's goal is to challenge those traditional orientations to provide new thematic categories. The main theme areas *Connecting Places, Connecting Things,* and *Connecting People,* each combine works of art from various cultural groups with the express intent of providing the visitor with ways to compare and look differently. The design of this exhibit consistently overturns traditional display concepts.

Connecting Places combines a visual background, replicating the lines from a map on display with paintings of mountains, oceans, and other scenic views. Each object appears on the map to subtly reflect the area it portrays. In the same section, a 12-foot tall shelf includes sculpted heads and statues of Buddha from around the world. The vertical integration of objects means that one can't really see the very top—which creates a certain level of intrigue (Figure 7.1). Nearby in the *Connecting People* section, an entire expanse of wall includes representations of people in paintings and sculptures from diverse ages and places. Throughout the space the goal is to make connections to the objects, across the objects, and with the objects. As a result, the "mix-up" gives the visitor an exciting orientation to look at objects in new ways. *Connecting Things* draws together several sets of objects including an expansive wall with small, open fronted boxes, each filled with a water pitcher. A very tall wall of mirrors alongside the boxes not only adds to the feel of the overall space but also adds the visitor's image as part of the *Connections.*

MAXIM 3. Be up front.

How can you help the visitor see what you want them to see? How can you let the visitor know that this experience is a partnership? How can you be trustworthy, transparent, and honest?

Many great writers, from Shakespeare to Mark Twain, have said, "Honesty is the best policy." If it worked for them, it can work for museums too. There's

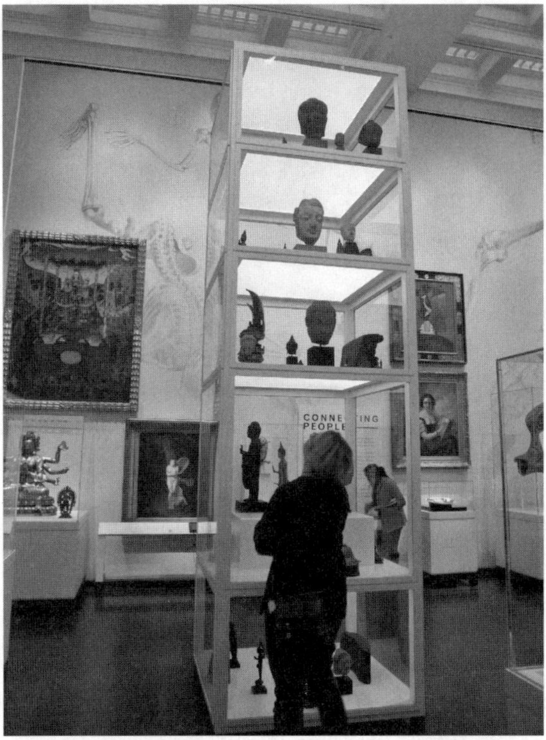

FIGURE 7.1 Breaking rules about "eye" level.
Photo by Kiersten F. Latham.

nothing wrong with being up front with visitors. Be honest with them; tell them why the museum included a particular object in the exhibition or program, or explain how they can use the information you present in their own lives. Principles of adult learning emphasize that people want to know how an experience will benefit their lives. Why not make suggestions, or create a conversation? Be direct, clear, and forthcoming about the experiences that visitors can have; help them understand the purpose and goals of an exhibit experience. Let them know who created the exhibit, where the information comes from, and why it is important.

Transparency in practice—not just in museums—is becoming more and more important in the 21st century. Being up front with how an exhibition or program was created, who was involved, and why it was created establishes the museum's stance and can help to redistribute power and authority. Unified visitor-object experiences come when people feel they have a role in making sense of an object or feel connected to it. An integral element of the Object Knowledge Framework is providing opportunities for visitors to contribute *their* knowledge or opinion of an object. Bringing visitor voice and knowledge into museum experiences helps form a partnership or a community between museum staff and visitors. While museum staff are still choosing the objects to be included in an exhibition or program, devising the experiences, and often still shaping the subject matter, why not tell it like it is? Tell visitors the big idea, tell them what they can get out of the exhibit, and tell them who the staff are and why they made the choices they did.

Being up front takes conscious effort. After all, museum people are trained to do seemingly mysterious things behind the scenes. It is easy to just get in a groove, do your work, and forget to stop and think about letting your visitors know how you got there. The following exercise is meant to help you stop and take stock during your process, to think about what you can, should, or would share with the visitor.

EXERCISE 9. *Revealing the Process*

Think about an object that you've included in an exhibit or program.

- Why did you include the object in the program or exhibit? What do you know about the object? How can you share that information with visitors? What else might they want to know?
- Visitors love to know about process and see what happens behind the scenes. Give them that chance. Think about how you can include information about how the team installs, cleans, cares for, and categorizes the object. Give them a chance to ask questions—and give them answers.
- What else is in the collection? What more can visitors see or find out from other sources?
- Tell the visitors about the people who work with the objects and details about their daily work.

WHAT DOES MAXIM 3 LOOK LIKE? **Doing the Housework in Public: *Fireworks of Glass*, The Children's Museum of Indianapolis.** Dale Chihuly's blown glass projects are as iconic as they are incredible. The sweeping, naturalistic shapes and bright colors are appealing in part because of their size, shape, and wild configurations. Many of his installations include enormous expanses of individual glass components, and they appear in a range of environments from outdoor sculpture and botanic gardens to art and children's museums. The *Fireworks of Glass* at The Children's Museum of Indianapolis rises up four stories through the museum's atrium. The 3,200 individually blown pieces of glass sit on top of a floor containing even more glass elements. Below this floor, visitors can sit on a rotating bench that allows them to look up into the ceiling just as though they were in a kaleidoscope.

What's "up front" about the *Fireworks of Glass*? Seeing the installation for the first time evokes a lot of visitor questions. How many pieces are there? How did they put it together? How do you clean it? Each of these questions is answered in one of the many text panels on the ramp that surrounds the sculpture. The information provided in the text panels gives many details about the process of making the glass and how the armature works. In addition, since it is pretty challenging to keep a Chihuly sculpture clean, workers dust the art in public during opening hours. It can be just as interesting to watch professionals rappel down the sculpture and clean each individual piece as it is to think about how the sculpture evokes the idea of fireworks.

WHAT DOES MAXIM 3 LOOK LIKE? **Seeing and Believing: *Luce Visible Storage*, The Metropolitan Museum of Art, New York, and Brooklyn Museum, Brooklyn, New York.** For many years, museum professionals have debated the merits of "visible storage"—a way to kill two birds with one stone, so to speak, by both storing collections and providing visitors a degree of access to more objects. In New York City, two prominent museums have dedicated space and funds to creating effective and interesting visible storage "exhibits." Through sponsorship from the Luce Foundation, both the Brooklyn Museum and the Metropolitan Museum of Art (Met) provide very modern and effective areas where a visitor can feel as if they are getting a behind-the-scenes tour, somewhat like making a "walk-in closet" for museums. Although the design of these areas emphasizes looking—with organizing labels and touch screen databases where one can look up objects—the areas are a stark contrast to the rest of the museums' exhibits, wherein objects are often more sparsely distributed, with large spaces between them, and expert interpretation shapes the visitor's experience with them. In the visible storage areas, a visitor chooses which objects to look for or to seek out.

The density of objects helps to demonstrate the vast numbers of things a museum might house in its collections. Walking through rows and rows of colored glass, of decorative arts, of paintings, sculpture, chairs, and more, visitors get a chance to see much of what typically remains hidden from view. This ability for museums to be more up front about the kinds of objects in their collections, or to demonstrate their strategies for storage, helps to reveal more of the museum's practices. At the Brooklyn Museum Visible Storage Center, the staff explicitly describes the purpose of the storage facility as a way to provide visitors with more access to objects. Wall text clarifies the intentional organization of the space, and the staff selection of special "focus objects" draws attention to interesting things within the collection. Within these visible storage facilities, the visitor also has access to the museum's catalog information on the object. When something catches the visitor's eye, the computer database provides more information for the visitor to access.

MAXIM 4. Don't forget simplicity and balance.

Can a simple strategy still have the same effect or outcome? Can I use the simple notion of balance to say things instead of other means, such as labels? How can the design use elegance to enhance the project?

It is easy to get caught up in all the details that go into an exhibition or program and forget that the same complicated concept could be said more simply or elegantly. In fact, human beings often communicate better when the message is simple. The principle of "Occam's Razor" says that when there are two competing theories that make exactly the same predictions, the simpler is the better. This principle has been in use since at least the 14th century and guides a whole range of innovations and inventions. Too much information or too many steps in a process can be very confusing, especially for museum visitors. This applies to both text and design concepts in exhibits and programs. Visitors do not always need every piece of background information on an object or a content area; sometimes spaces or gaps help inspire inquiry. Making careful selection of ideas, and "shaving away" what is unnecessary is a useful tool to help the idea of an object come to the forefront.

In concert with simplicity, understanding the role of balance is an important part of good, clear design. Balance is a *tool*, not a goal, something to be considered and manipulated as necessary. There are innumerable design challenges where *imbalance* is the correct solution to convey a given message. Neither is better or worse for communicating: they convey different things. In visual design, balance refers to the ways in which elements of something are arranged either *symmetrically* or *asymmetrically*. Symmetrical, or formal balance creates mirror images, whereas asymmetrical, or informal balance uses a variety of elements like color, shape, size and distance to create harmony in the visual field. Informal balance, while more difficult to achieve, helps to draw the visitor's attention to the message. In either case, good balance means that these elements work together to produce harmony overall. In short, balance and simplicity can communicate strong messages without saying a word.

The next two exercises are useful in helping the team sort out what layers of information may not be necessary or even are blocking the overall message.

EXERCISE 10. *Idea Balancing*

Look at your exhibit script or label text. What can you edit out while still conveying the same information? Can removing something actually make it better? Ask yourself:

- Are you forcing some idea? What can you minimize to make the idea fit better?
- How does the balance of the project communicate your ideas?
- What questions do you want visitors to have? Have you left spaces to allow for this?
- Which type of balance helps shape the transformation of objects in your project? In visual design, formal balance gives a feeling of stability and strength. Informal balance creates interest and excitement through tension. Radial balance, things moving around a central point, produces a sense of motion.

EXERCISE 11. *Idea Organizing*

Organization of ideas helps to simplify complicated concepts. What objects can be organized together to show the idea in another way? Try John Maeda's (2006) "SLIP" process:

- Write the name of all the objects and ideas connected to the project, each one on a separate slip of paper.
- Sort the pieces of paper into groups.
- Label each group.
- Integrate the objects and ideas in different groups into ideas that are essentially similar (yielding fewer groups).
- Prioritize the importance or role of these objects and concepts in relation to the big idea of the exhibit.
- Then, when you are finished, take a step back and review what you have. Are there things that can be removed or combined?

WHAT DOES MAXIM 4 LOOK LIKE? Simplicity and Balance in the Complex: *Spectrum of Life*, American Museum of Natural History, New York, New York. As part of the Biodiversity Hall, the *Spectrum of Life* (American Museum of Natural History, 2013) displays nearly 1,500 objects arranged in 28 different groupings, all of which contribute to the complex idea of the evolution of life on the planet Earth (Figure 7.2). This a nice example of simplicity and balance, not because of the vast numbers of objects included in the display but rather for the use of informal balance and the simplicity of the idea presented.

The asymmetrically balanced arrangement brings out a dynamic interaction between the objects that results in thought-provoking connections. How is the butterfly related to the giant spider crab? Where do plants fit in the larger scheme of life? The visual implications of the relationships between the objects are created through careful use of size, shape, color, and texture to create the vibrant mixture of life. The view itself is powerful and complex, yet uncluttered. Visually scanning the 100-foot-wide wall, visitors quickly see the relationship between large and small creatures. An arc of seeds from the most diminutive to the largest pinecone spreads across the wall. A butterfly arrangement makes it appear as though they are soaring in flight. Every inch of the visual spectrum uses balance to create provocative images that stimulate curiosity and awe.

The display presents a "spectrum" of life as a visual continuum of plants, animals, and insects. Rather than complicating the visual field with text information or attempting to make connections between the various flora and fauna, the design allows the visitor to focus wherever she or he likes. The text and information are still present, just off to the side and below the displays. The organization of ideas is what helps make the overall experience simple.

Transforming through Design Takeaways

Design for an exhibition or program draws on team collaboration to create environments that stimulate unified visitor-object experiences. Each of the four maxims of design focuses attention on ways to enhance the visitor experience with objects. The transformation of objects through daring, imaginative organization, balance, and simplicity can stimulate feelings and emotions in visitors. Design creates moments for identification with an idea or concept. Thinking carefully about the "rules" that guide practices, and which ones can be bent or broken in the spirit of providing intuitive and

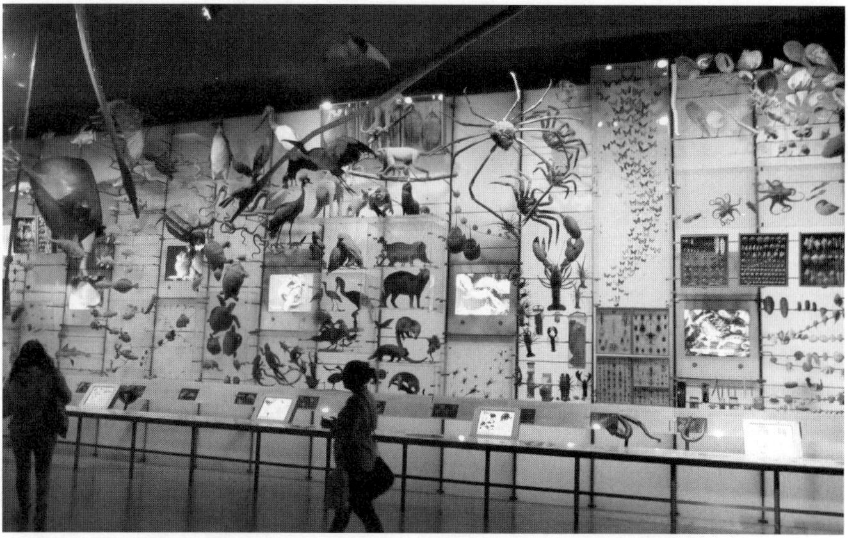

FIGURE 7.2 Balance, symmetry, and asymmetry. Photo by Elee Wood.

inclusive experiences, helps to create better connections between visitor and object. Being up front about practices, about expectations and about information is part of a design strategy that raises the authority of the visitor to a new level.

While design itself is not just about the visual or aesthetic elements of an exhibition or program, understanding the fundamentals of design and the role of design in bringing objects into a project is critical. The ultimate goal in the transformation of objects through design is in showing or revealing, through visual, organizational, and non-verbal means, how visitors can see the object in different contexts.

CHAPTER EIGHT

Transformation through Content

While the design maxims ask the question, "How do I show or reveal the object to help the visitor to make a connection?" achieving transformation in terms of content means focusing on the ways that museum staff draw out messages and information contained within and around the world of the object. In this chapter we emphasize the idea that objects are the key content of an exhibition or program. The goal for a transformation through content asks the question, "What do I want to share with or say to the visitor about the object?" The content and its message help create context and connections between the objectworld and the visitor lifeworld. The next four maxims (5 to 8) highlight strategies to draw out elements of the object's presence in the world and its possible meanings. The intent is not to eliminate content expertise or interpretation and let objects speak for themselves. Instead, it is about balancing the knowledge that curators and other museum experts have about the objects and what visitors want to know. It is also about using objects and object-based experiences to connect visitors to the exhibition message or program information. In a sense, the curatorial team acts as information brokers about the object.

For every object there is a sphere of information that surrounds it. This objectworld includes all the actions, people, events, and information related to the object before it came to be in the museum; behind the object is something like the "contrail" that remains in the sky even after a plane is long gone. An object has the same kind of path, and a history from before its life in the museum. Eventually the visual evidence of the trail disappears, but the information can still be found. The more that museums can unlock this history and share some of that pathway with visitors, including the object's life in the museum itself, the more they will be able to help visitors make connections to the object.

Elizabeth Wood and Kiersten F. Latham, "Transformation through Content" in *The Objects of Experience: Transforming Visitor-Object Encounters in Museums*, pp 132-147.

Visitor-object encounters are the drivers of museum experiences. In extracting the content messages—the ideas and information from objects—visitors can and will make any number of interpretations on their own. This does not take the place of a curator's expertise or the deep knowledge that museum staff have around the object. Instead, it is about inviting visitors to share their knowledge and insight about objects too. For example, *Gallery One* at the Cleveland Museum of Art in Ohio integrates a variety of interactive "lenses" that invite visitor contributions on the meaning of art (Figure 8.1). In the "Lion Lens" visitors review the meaning and symbolism around different depictions of a lion and then vote on different interpretations. A display of results shows visitors how their vote compares with others. Alongside are labels and other information provided through museum staff research. This activity demonstrates the successful combination of expert content in the curated artworks related to lions with user-generated content on the meaning of lion.

In shaping and integrating an object into the storyline and narrative of an exhibition or program, museums provide visitors with a new way to connect their own lifeworld with that of the objectworld. Throughout this book we have described the effects that physical things have in shaping our world; the four maxims discussed in this chapter provide strategies to bring visitors into settings where the content connections with objects might support a unified experience.

MAXIM 5. An Object is Worth 1,000 Meanings.

What objects are connected to your ideas? What ideas are connected to your objects? What are the visitor connections to objects? What meaning do visitors already have about the objects?

One of the most important findings of the research presented in this book is that there is much more to any object than one might expect. People make connections to all kinds of objects in innumerable ways. Being able to draw out these meanings is a critical strategy in building transformations for visitors. Objects—whether they are artifacts, specimens, artwork, or props—are an integral part of exhibitions and programs that provide tremendous opportunities to communicate content. Museum projects traditionally use objects as examples of ideas, or as illustrations of concepts. Instead, try treating the object *as the content of* the project. In doing so, museum staff can develop new ways to identify, select, or use objects to reinforce ways that visitors can contribute to the range of meanings and interpretations of ideas.

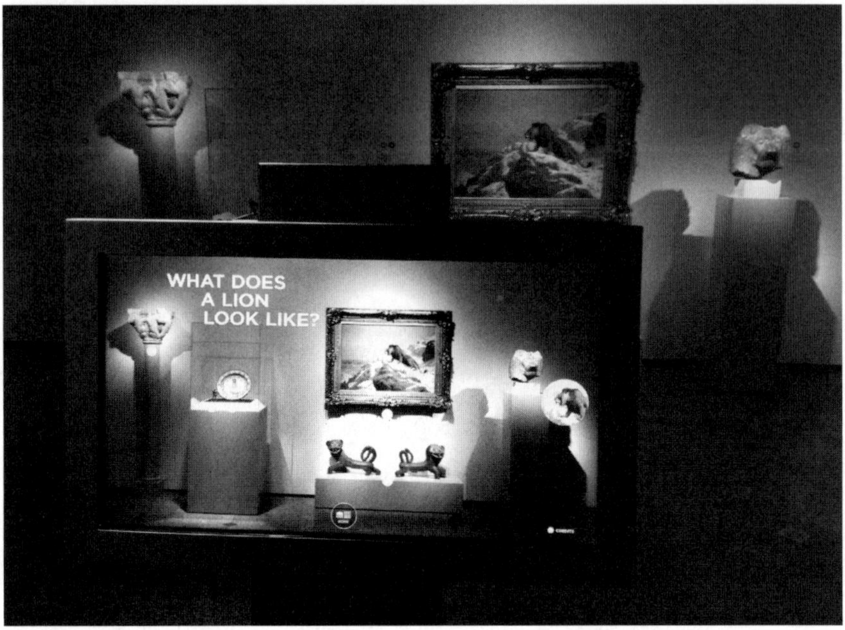

FIGURE 8.1 Different lenses for Lions. Photo by Kiersten F. Latham.

The following exercises are both fun and informative. They are simple enough to do with several objects or just one object that may be central to your concept, or even with several to help sort out which objects may best play a role in the project. Both exercises can aid in drawing out the multiple meanings that surround a single object and help enrich the team process around creating exhibits and programs.

EXERCISE 12. *The Many-Faceted Piece of Cloth*

To stimulate thinking about the potential meaning that can come from objects, here's an activity from our theatre colleagues to get ideas flowing. It would be best to start first with a generic item, such as a piece of cloth, before moving to the intended exhibition objects. This can be done in a group or on your own. Start with a sizeable length of plain cloth, such as a white or neutral cotton tablecloth or piece of muslin. As quickly as possible, pass the cloth around from person to person. Each person takes the cloth and transforms it into as many different concepts as possible. A key goal for conducting this activity is to demonstrate the message or content of the object by acting it out rather than speaking aloud. Try to show at least five different ways the cloth might be used. For example, a piece of cloth can become a blanket, a shawl, or a towel, but it might also be transformed into a ball, a tightrope, or a swimming pool. Though this exercise may seem pointless at first, it is amazing to see the number of ideas that can come from a concerted effort to look for meaning. When applied to the museum context, the activity provides avenues to think broadly about what objects can say or do, especially when considering objects destined for an exhibition. This improvisational process helps museum staff acknowledge both what they already know about an object and other potential meanings, through movement and kinesthetic interpretation.

EXERCISE 13. *The Many-Faceted Object*

Begin with an object you intend to include in the exhibition. Rather than handling the object, as with the cloth, place it in a location where the team has access to look at it and, if permitted, investigate the object thoroughly. Leave it out for a length of time. Perhaps leave paper and pencils nearby for staff to record reactions. By starting with the object, you begin to think about what the object means from a whole range of perspectives.

Ask the following questions:

- What does this mean from the perspectives of history, art, economics, geography, the sciences, culture, psychology, literature, religion, etc.?
- Who might have used this object? How does that change the object's meaning or purpose?
- How has the object been used through time? Where or when does the meaning of the object change? Why?
- How can this object communicate an idea or message?
- What material qualities might intersect with other perspectives?
- How might the object surprise visitors? What stories might they not know?
- What aspects of the object will draw the visitor closer?
- How might the object reveal or expose a hidden secret?

WHAT DOES MAXIM 5 LOOK LIKE? **Good, Bad, or Indifferent? *Controversy,* The Ohio Historical Society, Columbus, Ohio.** In 2011, the staff at the Ohio Historical Society in Columbus, Ohio, wanted to experiment with museum objects by letting visitors have more say in the meaning made through a museum exhibition. They delved into their permanent collections to find provocative objects that "ignited real, raw emotion" (Ohio Historical Society, 2013). The result was *Controversy: Pieces You Don't Normally See.* Curators placed five objects in the exhibition—a Ku Klux Klan robe, a sheepskin condom, a human cage, an electric chair, and a thumb mitt (to prevent thumb sucking)—each in its own room with only a single small label with minimal description (e.g., "Electric Chair"). Visitors were able to let their own thoughts filter through about each object, rather than being guided by an external voice. Then, at the end of the exhibition visitors could express themselves through various means and review "curator books" filled with the results of rich research, images, statistics, contemporary newspapers, documents, and other information about each object. Following a brief introduction of the goals of the exhibition, visitors entered the space using only their lifeworld knowledge (the individual, group, and material dimensions) to make sense of the objects on display. The individual visitor made her own meaning of each object she encountered.

The exhibition design was integral to this experience but so too was the ability of the curators to "pull back" and leave the objects un-interpreted beyond the selection, placement, and choice of label text. Each object was placed in the center of its own room, so that a visitor could walk all the way around it. The rooms were quiet and simple, painted charcoal grey with lighting focused pointedly onto each object. In the far corners of each room were short description labels placed a distance from the object. At the end of the five rooms, visitors entered a large space filled with a range of ways to express and communicate about what they had just seen. They could write or draw their thoughts on overhead projectors, or sit on a bank of stools at a counter to write postcards or spend time with the curator books about each object. The inclusion of this information after the presentation of objects provided the staff with an opportunity to extend their views on the objects and present visitors with information that they may not have known. In addition, there were benches for sitting, contemplation, rest, or conversation.

Removing the curatorial voice early in the exhibition and simplifying the display stripped the objects of a traditional "interpretation" strategy through text. Instead, the transformation of the objects, particularly by removing much of their context and history, led to visitor discussion and observation of the objects. In this way visitors had to draw on much of their own individual, material, and group knowledge of the things they saw. For some, this was a challenging perspective to take; for others, especially those who were less aware of the history, context, or use of the object, their perceptions may have led to a wide range of assumptions. In the end, using the objects as content had powerful effects on the audience.

MAXIM 6. Make it personal.

How can you help the visitor connect personally to this object? How can the visitor feel that this is their object? How does this object matter from other viewpoints or other experiences?

Customization, whether of objects or learning, drives much of the design of experience in contemporary society (Pine & Gilmore, 1999). Personalization in museums is possible if the visitor's knowledge and experience become part of the equation that museum staff use for designing projects. Experiences can involve creativity, real-life connections, and ownership of ideas. Museums can excel in creating opportunities for people of all backgrounds, learning styles, and knowledge if this process is done thoughtfully. To do so requires relinquishing a little bit of authority on the museum side of things, while at the same time building opportunities for the visitor to contribute some of their own knowledge and ideas.

Creating a personal experience with an object is one of the major goals of the Object Knowledge Framework. When a visitor has an opportunity to make that connection, it leads toward the goal of a unified experience. The ways that museums make objects personal can be something as simple as adding a label that poses a question about the visitor's point of view or might include an opportunity to vote on a meaning. The Columbus Museum of Art in Ohio provides a great example. They host a small, changing thematic exhibit called *Curious Collections,* which consists of three cases in an otherwise nondescript hallway. During "Shiny," the three cases were the "Museum Edition" (objects from the museum's collections), "Staff Edition" (objects from staff's private collections), and "Visitor Edition" (objects that visitors left to be displayed). The visitor case had small shelves where people dug into their purses or pockets to leave something "shiny" to be displayed at the museum. Involving visitors in the exhibit itself, and even encouraging them to leave their own things behind, creates personalized connections that help visitors make sense of their own experiences and can promote dialogue and reflection.

In the course of this book, we have mentioned many times the importance of the individual dimension—in relation to the other dimensions, to other people, to objects, and more. Here we offer an activity to collect visitor points of view on objects that can inform strategies for personalization of the object.

EXERCISE 14. *If You Owned the Object*

Generate a list of the specific objects intended for inclusion in the exhibition. Take the objects out into the museum and gather some comments from visitors. Designate members of the team to interview visitors and others to observe the visitors and objects.

- Ask each visitor to describe an experience they had with the object, their ideas about what is important, and how they might feel connected to the object. Gather as much detail as you can. You might ask things like:
  - — What does this object remind you of? Does it relate to anything in your own life?
  - — Is this object similar to something you've seen before? How similar or different is it?
  - — If you had an object like this, what features would help you know that it was yours? What about that makes it important to you?
  - — Where would you put this in your home? How would you display it? What else would go with it?
  - — Would it have a special place in your home? Do you think you would use or show it for special occasions or all the time? Would you point it out to others who visit?
- Review the responses collected. Organize the ideas into categories. What kinds of features or ideas about the object did people talk about?
- Compare the visitor responses with the planned exhibit messages. What information is missing? What are the differences between the plan for the exhibition and the visitors' ideas? How might this make a difference for the goals of the project?
- Finally, think about a way that visitors might be able to personalize their experience with the object. Is there something they can add or contribute to the object or its display? What might the visitor leave behind?
- How will the visitor make it their own?

WHAT DOES MAXIM 6 LOOK LIKE? Personal Perspectives and *Forces of Change*, Oakland Museum of California, Oakland, California. As part of the *History of California* exhibition at the Oakland Museum of California, museum staff invited visitors and friends of the museum to help them explain the significant societal changes that occurred between 1960 and 1975. An introductory label accompanying the exhibition says, "We at the Oakland Museum of California felt it was impossible to sum up this period just by ourselves. Instead, we invited 24 Californians to turn their memories into the displays that surround you—24 different perspectives about these times" (Oakland Museum, 2012).

Each person created a small 3' x 2' diorama that included objects, documents, and visual images relating to their experiences between 1960 and 1975. Along with each diorama is a personal statement and interpretation of the vignette from the guest curator. The themes and ideas cover a wide spectrum of experiences representing small town life, politics and political involvement, popular culture of children and youth, as well as prominent civic and cultural events. Many of the objects are very personal, and yet stepping back into the other parts of this exhibition on California history, one readily sees that these objects are just as valuable and important as those selected by the museum's curators.

Clearly woven throughout the gallery itself is the attention given to personal connections and ideas related to objects of history. What's more, this display will change every two years to include more and more voices. Not only does this reflect a powerful display of personalized meaning and connection to history, it also reflects Maxim 3, "Be up front."

WHAT DOES MAXIM 6 LOOK LIKE? "Sit Here": Open Doors: *If These Walls Could Talk*, Minnesota Historical Society, St. Paul, Minnesota. A challenge for many historical museums is making history more relatable to everyday life. When the Minnesota Historical Society decided to demonstrate the idea of change over time in of one of St. Paul's neighborhoods, the team decided to share the history of all the residents of a single, actual house over the course of 100 years (Filene, 2011). Their achievements in developing the exhibition led to unique interactive opportunities in the re-creation of the house. Each re-created room of the "house" highlights the story of a different family in a different time period. Starting in the living room with the earliest inhabitants, the exhibition moves through the kitchen, dining room, bedrooms, and backyard, giving the visitor a full circle experience of time and space that helps to put a very personal spin on each family. Clever integrations of stories from oral history research appear throughout the "house." Furthermore, each story connects to a specific object in each room. Although these objects are replicas, using three-dimensional objects to tell a story is fundamental to the overall strategy of the exhibition. As the tales unfold in each room, the objects take on a central role in supporting the visitor interaction with the story and ultimately help to draw the visitor's own experiences into the narrative. For instance, as visitors enter one of the bedrooms, they see the words "sit here" projected onto the bed, inviting the visitors to sit on the bed. As they do, an audio recording begins to tell the story of the bed and how it continually fell apart at the most inconvenient times. At that moment in the story, the bed where visitors are sitting collapses—with the visitors sitting on it! In the kitchen, cranking the sausage grinder reveals a story, as each sausage link comes out the end. These actions, the presence of objects, and the connection to stories demonstrate the personal link that people have with objects. While the exhibit obviously does not contain the exact same things that the visitors might have in their own homes—or even those that were in the original house that the exhibit is about—the stories and the objects make the personal connection.

MAXIM 7. **Leave room for more.**

What can visitors fill in for themselves? What can (or should) be left unsaid? How can we create spaces, gaps, or openings on purpose?

One of the most valuable aspects of working in a museum setting is the vast potential of information available to share with visitors. The good news is that not all of this information needs to be conveyed. "Leaving room for more" is similar to Maxim 6, Make it Personal, in that there is always a way to let the visitor fill in what they know about something. By providing just enough information to stimulate experiences and interest in an object, museum staff leave space for the visitor to contribute to ideas, shape the experience further, and pursue more information on their own. Not only does an open-ended experience provide more opportunity for the visitor to "fill in the blanks," but it also provides the visitor a role in determining what works best for their curiosity and attention. Leaving room for more allows museum staff to guide content ideas and inquiry. Whether the approach to the exhibition or program is dialogic (as a conversation), guided by questions that ask visitors to tackle enduring, unanswerable questions about human life, or whether it simply invites making connections across a wide range of topics, there is always room for the visitor's voice in the experience.

How can we know where to leave an opening? Let's face it: we now live in a world awash in information. At any time, if we have a smart phone or a tablet, we can look up the answers to our questions. Adding to this, there are likely to be visitors who actually want more information immediately, and it is important to keep options available for them by helping them find more information or providing it in an alternate medium or location. Even so, people still make their own meanings out of what they see in museums. The exercises that follow provide a couple of ways to think about creating gaps, leaving room for the visitor to fill in more for himself.

EXERCISE 15. *Tweet Your Label*

In order to leave room for more, the best strategy is to condense the amount of information. This doesn't mean reducing the importance of the information, but rather communicating your ideas in a different way.

- Condense the text or label for an object into 140 characters (including all spaces and punctuation), the same length as the microblogging platform Twitter uses.
- Try writing information about the object in the form of a haiku: 5 syllables in one line, 7 syllables in the second, and 5 syllables in the third.
- Try replacing some of the words with symbols or images.
- After each iteration of the label, look at how each of these strategies informs the meaning. What has to stay? What can go?

EXERCISE 16. *One Plus None, One Plus One*

Imagine putting the object in a blank space. Then add just one object that will provide context. Try this multiple times. What differences happen with adding just one object? What kinds of objects enhance the story? What happens to the story? Imagine that visitors can add one object of their own. How does this help to tell the story?

WHAT DOES MAXIM 7 LOOK LIKE? **Opening Doors to Imagination: Lower Eastside Tenement Museum, New York.** Without question, the histories of the residents from the Lower Eastside Tenement Museum don't really work as well without the building's physical presence. Even though the accounts told here are about the everyday lives of the many people who inhabited it, the building itself brings the former residents to life. The museum excels in the way it tells those stories in the context of the physical structure. Visitors can only see the structure inside by taking a tour. The tour design allows visitors to create meaning and value by filling in the details as they move through the space itself—the same space where these actual historical people once moved.

The nature of the tours is dialogic, based on questions to the participants, and in turn, this questioning strategy brings forth more information and ideas than one would get from a traditional label. For example, in the entryway of the entire building, before the tour really starts, the guide instructs participants to stop and think about what it would be like walking up the stairs each day. The questions that can emerge—"Who lived here? Was her life like mine? Where did she go?"—linger in the air, in the silence the tour guide allows.

Every inch of the building has a tale to tell, but that story is not always the one the tour guide shares. On each tour, the participants only hear one part of the building's history, and about just one or two of the families who dwelt there. This kind of open-ended experience provides an important opportunity to build on the visitor's own life experiences, as well as the shared experiences of the group dimension. Throughout the tour, the guide shares small details about objects to reinforce and reiterate several of the storylines. "Hold Julia's iron."... "This room is re-created based on Josefina's oral history" down to the placement of the Linnit soap and the Bon Ami cleanser on the kitchen sink. Each of these details draws out thoughts about what life might have been like at that time and leaves the visitor imagining all kinds of possibilities.

MAXIM 8. **It's all connected.**

What web of connections surrounds an object? What links to other subjects can an object reveal? What can they conceal? How can you integrate multiple disciplines into the idea?

In the late 1970s, science historian James Burke created a television series called *Connections*. The premise of the show was that innovations and inventions of the modern world were the result of a series of interconnected events. He traced the relational path of things like the evolution of telecommunications to stirrups on a saddle; the changes from one innovation in something like warfare led to a massive change in how people communicate across the world. The message was clear—nothing happens in isolation. When you start to think about it, everything is connected to everything else. History, art, and science all intersect in some way or another, and yet over time these have evolved into distinctive fields and we now often continue to keep them separate, by tradition more than anything else. Bringing the seemingly disparate ideas of art and science, history and technology, or other disciplinary combinations back together provides museum visitors with a better view of how things really work. The world is really a giant web of interconnecting parts within which sits the object. The way in which the museum presents elements of the object's world through design elements, content, and activities helps visitors make stronger connections to themselves, to their world. There are many connections to be made and visitors will do this naturally; it is even better when the exhibition or program can do it too.

EXERCISE 17. *Five Whys*

This is a classic activity for finding cause and effect relationships like those presented in this maxim. This activity explores the *relationships* between the project ideas and the visitor's worldview.

To start, think about an object included in the project. Working with the project team, begin by asking the question, Why is this important? Then, use the responses to refine the meaning. Each time you ask the question, go deeper into the previous answers, working to arrive at the core idea. This process of probing for root causes and origins of an idea will create the connections between the ideas and the bigger picture. Think about the larger (and smaller) implications of your ideas.

EXAMPLE. **A historic child's pull toy in a preschool exhibition**

FIRST WHY: Why is this object important?

ANSWER: It connects to the parents.

> **SECOND WHY:** Why is it important to connect to parents?
>
> **ANSWER:** We want parents to be stimulated by something that they can relate to.
>
> > **THIRD WHY:** Why do we want to stimulate parents?
> >
> > **ANSWER:** So that parents see themselves in the exhibition.
> >
> > > **FOURTH WHY:** Why should they see themselves in an exhibition for toddlers?
> > >
> > > **ANSWER:** To help them make a stronger connection between themselves and their children, and hopefully talk to their children.
> > >
> > > > **FIFTH WHY:** Why are those connections important?
> > > >
> > > > **ANSWER:** Because we know that when parents interact with young children, especially verbally, it stimulates brain development.

By the time the team arrives at the fifth "why" the answers begin to demonstrate the connections between the big idea of the exhibit and the role of the objects. This exercise is a useful test to uncover some of the hidden ideas that might lurk within an exhibit concept, or to reveal the strength of the connections between the ideas and objects.

WHAT DOES MAXIM 8 LOOK LIKE? **Typology in the 21st Century: Pitt Rivers Museum, Oxford, England.** The Pitt Rivers Museum, part of the University of Oxford and founded in 1884, is a classic example of late 19th century museum practices, featuring collections of anthropological and archaeological materials. The objects are organized according to typologies such as "treatment of the dead" or "objects made of bone and ivory," and for all appearances look as though they are crammed and jammed into cases as old as the museum. But, interestingly, the Pitt Rivers staff undertook a major transformation of their interpretation of the objects in the museum in 2006 (Figure 8.2). The museum's initial concept of organizing objects by type for comparison across cultures was popular at the time, but this interpretation positions the museum in an "us and them" orientation to other cultures, a stance that is considered old fashioned in the museum and scientific world. As part of a multi-year initiative, the museum staff began a process to re-shape and re-position the interpretation of the objects toward a cross- or trans –cultural view of the world (Pitt Rivers, 2012), all while continuing to maintain the historically important museal character of the museum. This new emphasis meant maintaining some of the historical elements of the displays like the handwritten labels and density of objects in the display cases, but also some newer elements such as the introductory labels that provide context and guidance for viewing the objects.

The value of the museum's organization and displays is in the meaning derived from seeing many objects that cut across time, geography, and culture. This orientation provides greater opportunity for visitors to see and make the connections between themselves and the objects, and see the object in other cultures and aspects of human life. It also connects the past with today in a multitude of ways. Witnessing objects of cultures now long-gone or changed, a 21st century visitor also can sense what it must have felt like to see an exhibit in the 19th century museum.

WHAT DOES MAXIM 8 LOOK LIKE? **Historic Objects Inspire Art: *Camp Arty-Fact*, Kentucky Historical Society, Lexington, Kentucky.** Being flexible with content, thinking big, and working across ideas can be challenging—

in any kind of museum. At the Kentucky Historical Society (KHS), Camp ArtyFact is a series of programs that bring together art making and history through a series of camps for children ages 5 to 12. By drawing on themes and objects from their permanent collection, the education staff created a unique and fun experience for kids that uses history as inspiration for self-designed art projects and experiences. KHS staff used examples from the museum's collection and the Society's library, museum, and historic site to support participants in creating their own works of art.

One of the programs, *Build, Build, BUILD,* explores a range of historic architecture and bridge-building techniques so that kids can create their own structures. First, the campers visit the KHS library to have a hands-on experience with an extensive historic postcard collection. During their visit, the camper's goal is to look through the postcards to find historic architectural bridge designs to inform their own creations. Each camper gets to peruse a box of postcards from the library's extensive collection. The librarian instructs them on how to best handle and use the postcards—and then they are off on their own to explore and discover. The campers select a few options, make notes and sketches, and then take these back to make their own building and bridge.

In another program of the camp, *Secret Identities and Alter Egos,* young children explore the stories of Civil War-era spies and then create their own disguises based on mask-making and theater exercises. They also discuss the dress of everyday people of the past and of statesmen, based on observations of paintings and portraits from the time. During a culminating event, they use their spy skills including map reading, and sneaking around and hiding, derived from Kentucky frontiersmen, to find a hidden object in the Old State Capitol without getting caught. They celebrate their success with a gala in the Old State Capitol rotunda with a dance party. The combination of theater and history brings to light the importance of the objects that give life, shape, and context to the program.

What is unique about *Camp ArtyFact* is the attention that staff put on the development of thematic and cross-disciplinary content to help engage children in history through the use of objects. The camp goals are to connect participant interests with the resources and collections of the institution. Classes are designed around the collection, and the arts are a vehicle to connect with the participants. The process of building these camps allows staff to draw on the importance of using and accessing primary sources. The camp programs and the access to objects create an opportunity for staff to share the museum's expertise and for young people to share in the creation

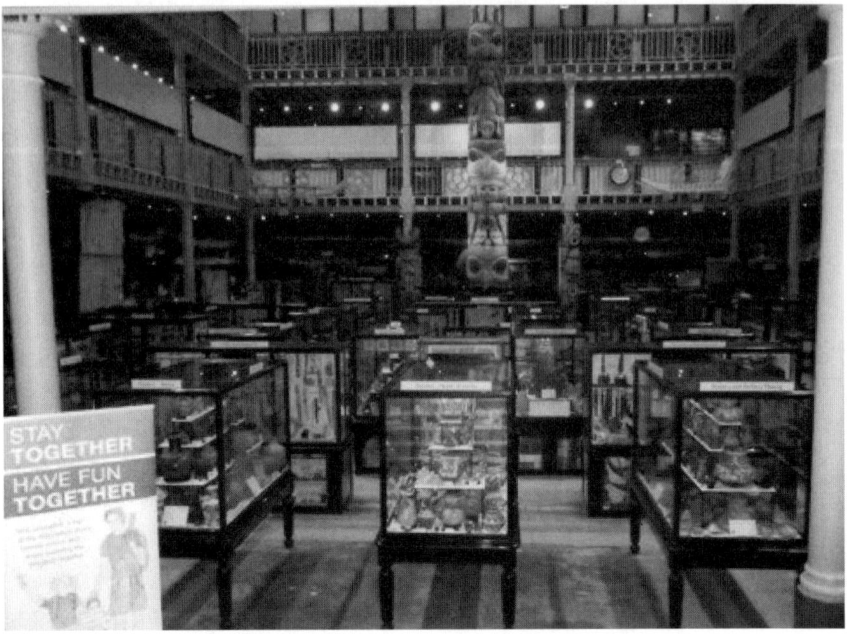

FIGURE 8.2 The Pitt Rivers Museum. Photo by Kiersten F. Latham.

of new ideas. Young people leave camp with an interconnected view of history through their experiences using the arts.

Transformation through Content Takeaways

Objects form the basis for most museum content, even if they are not part of a museum's collection. The presence of objects helps visitors make links between information and their own experiences. By bringing visitors and objects into closer proximity, the potential exists for greater unified experiences. Each object yields the potential for as many meanings as there are visitors to the museum. By acknowledging and shaping exhibition and program content along these lines, museum staff support greater personal connections and interactions with objects.

The extent of these ideas does not need to be all encompassing. The more that museum staff think intentionally about the ways in which objects represent content, the more room there is for visitor contribution of ideas, which ultimately leads visitors to absorb more of the provided information. Rather than putting the burden on the visitor to take in too much information, more can be accomplished by leaving things unsaid, or leaving it open for more interpretation or investigation by the visitor. More importantly, by serving as advocates for object-related content information, museum staff can find ways to connect with the things that visitors want to know. Finally, making links across multiple content areas and disciplines helps to demonstrate the more realistic, interconnected world that people live in. All of these approaches to content make for greater potential to connect object content to the individual experience of the visitor.

CHAPTER NINE

Transformation through Participation

The final component for Transforming Objects into Experiences is participation. The goal here is to ask the question, "What do I want the visitor to actually *do* with this object?" Establishing conditions where visitors are *actively engaged* within exhibitions and programs involves planning for situations in which the visitor's involvement with an object represents their own contribution, allows for sharing, or is directed toward addressing their interests. In doing this, museum staff can ask: What roles do visitors play in shaping the experience of the object for themselves? How many ways can a person experience an object? What does this exhibition mean personally to this visitor? How can the visitor become actively involved?

Active learning situations, wherein the visitor joins the process through their senses, their intellect, and their emotions, all aid in the development of unified experiences. More and more museums are developing opportunities for actual touching and handling of original objects. These are exceptional moments that can result in heightened sensory-based encounters with objects. Participation is more than just handling objects, however; the involvement of visitors, cognitively and emotionally as well as physically, is key to opening avenues to meaningful encounters with objects. The idea of "scaffolding" is a principle in educational theory that helps the learner accomplish a task on her own. In the museum setting, this scaffolding process comes from providing multiple ways of conveying the same information for a wide range of visitors. Multisensory and multimodal communication strategies support a visitor's opportunity for success in knowing more about the exhibit or program elements. Museum staff can use this approach to develop the project context in ways that cultivate the connections that visitors can have. Scaffolding is possible when the planning team makes intentional choices about the direction and goals of the experience with an eye toward visitor participation.

Elizabeth Wood and Kiersten F. Latham, "Transformation through Participation" in *The Objects of Experience: Transforming Visitor-Object Encounters in Museums*, pp 148-162.

The last four maxims (9 to 12) build on increasing the engagement between people and objects that we described in Maxims 1 to 8. By incorporating multiple ways of understanding the same object, museum staff create more possibilities for people to connect to objects, making the objects themselves more enticing and exciting. When visitors make these connections, they are more likely to reach greater heights in their views of the world and their place in it. Creating a rich visitor experience starts with thinking about these kinds of visitor reactions.

MAXIM 9. The physical matters.

How does the physical presence of the object affect the visitor experience? What information, experience, or feeling does it reveal beyond what the museum provides? What sensory aspects of the object can visitors access?

In Section Two, our research on person-object encounters reiterated that the actual, solid presence of the three-dimensional object, taking up space within proximity of the person, provides multiple levels of meaning and emotional connections. Museum professionals often wonder whether there is a difference in visitor experience between a "real" thing (the original object) and a replica (a copy of the original). Depending on the message of the program or exhibition, one may do the job just fine over the other. However, knowing how the physical presence of the object supports the visitor encounter helps museum staff to plan for appropriate experiences. Sometimes the real thing matters a great deal in the message of the exhibition or project; at other times, a replica is a useful alternative when the ideas need to be illustrated. Both the real thing and the replica are physical, manipulable, and present in the moment, and often this presence and solid representation helps people make connections between ideas and objects.

Beyond the physical, tangible presence of the object is the sensory role that an object plays in an encounter. Sensory experiences are significant components of human learning that can get overlooked in project planning, yet they are often conduits to profound human emotion and understanding. Even though most museums have a good handle on how to deal with the visual features of objects, other senses like smell, sound, and touch are typically only used in science and children's museums. And more, sensory experiences in museums can even go beyond the classic five senses: building relationships with objects can provide sensations of healing and pain, time and spatial relations, movement and direction, and temperature, to name just a few. By uniting these sensorial activities with the presence of an object, museum staff can build platforms for unified experiences.

Many museum staff have created "hands-on" components for exhibits or programs. But how can these kind of activities go farther to allow for active engagement with objects? How can museum exhibitions become the platform for unified experiences between people and objects? This exercise goes through a purposeful exploration of the multiple ways visitors could physically interact with a particular object.

EXERCISE 18: *Getting Engaged with…*

Consider an object or set of objects. Using the following sensory ideas, generate words or visual cues that could help the visitor connect the material qualities of the object and their personal experiences. With the objects in front of you, explore them (as much as possible) through these different channels. Smell them, turn them upside down and look at the bottom, listen to them, see them in another context.

Then ask yourself, how could the visitor engage with the object through:

- **Senses:** sight, smell, touch, taste, hearing?
- **Space:** movement, direction, placement?
- **Sound:** loud, soft, clear, muffled, augmented, altered?
- **Time:** the past, the present, the future?

Other Senses: empathy, connection, love, pain, hope, healing? Try writing a label for the object for each of these sensory categories. Play different kinds of music during different "visits." Compile the labels and put them in front of the objects and have the team "visit the exhibit." Discuss your reactions to the object and labels. Did anything surprise you? Did the focus on other senses give you new information about the object? Consider how you might incorporate these experiences into the exhibit or program.

WHAT DOES MAXIM 9 LOOK LIKE? **Hearing First Contact: *Coming to California,* Oakland Museum of California, Oakland, California.** As part of a museum-wide re-interpretation of galleries and collections, the Oakland Museum of California's exhibition, *Coming to California,* provides first-hand accounts and experiences of history. Drawing on both contemporary and historic narratives, the exhibition highlights the experiences of Native people, both past and present, as well as the numerous stories of immigrants, settlers, and colonizers, and the interactions among all of them. What is notable about this exhibit is its use of quotes, both through the text and audio components—rather than extensive didactic text —to explain and enhance the interpretive message. In many of the exhibit areas, recordings of people's voices and stories augment the presence of the object. Along the way, objects illustrate and echo storylines to provide authority to the message while reinforcing the role of objects within the personal experience. For example, an exhibit section called "Encuentro de Cultura (Cultures Meet)" is an examination of first contact between Native people and Spanish colonists solely through the use of objects. Two headpieces, a helmet and a feather topknot, are positioned individually in cases slightly below eye-level (Figure 9.1). Lighting highlights each headpiece and an audio track plays a hypothetical conversation between the two. There are, importantly, no text panels in the room. The dialogue emphasizes the differences in language between the two cultures and helps draw out, and perhaps even reveal, the vast differences that exist even to this day. In this small component of the exhibition, the curators position universal themes of discovery against the imagined moment of encounter between two groups of people. The global implications of colonialism and conquest of Native tribes are clearly represented through the selection of objects. At the same time, the objectworlds of both items is represented through the audio track, as well as the careful placement of the headpieces at equal levels. The presence of the physical objects, as well as the audio surrounding them, illustrates the complex idea presented in the exhibition through tangible, physical things, as well as many fine examples of transformation through the design.

WHAT DOES MAXIM 9 LOOK LIKE? The Power of the Real Thing: *America's Smithsonian*, Smithsonian Institution, Washington, District of Columbia

In the late 1990s, the Smithsonian traveled a two-year exhibit of 300 of the nation's treasures. Called *America's Smithsonian*, the museum presented this show to the public in twelve major cities across the United States. Examples of things that were shown are Abraham Lincoln's hat, the Apollo 11 spacecraft, Dizzy Gillespie's trumpet, and Dorothy's ruby slippers. Over and over, people were awestruck by the power of the exhibit and, in more than a few cases, were found weeping before the cases of objects. Kurin (1997), writing about the overwhelming reactions to this traveling exhibit, commented:

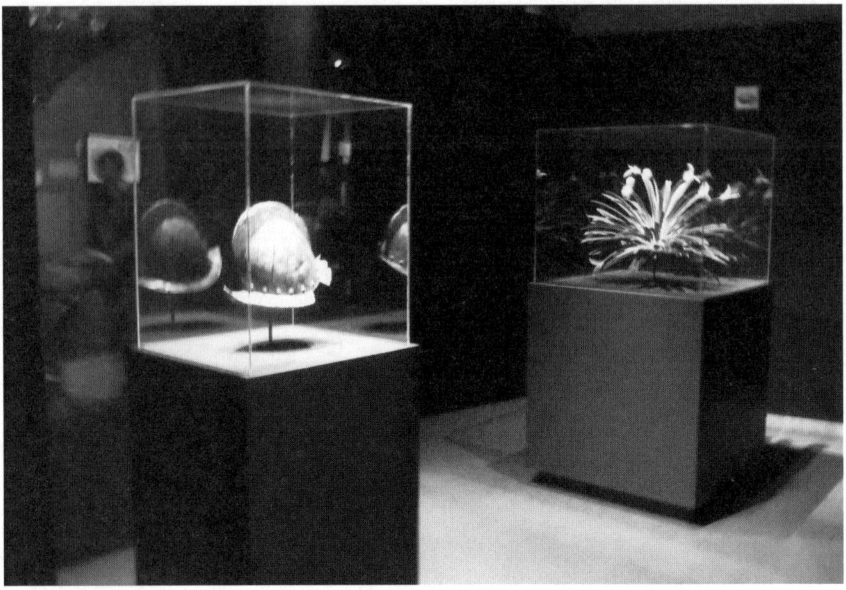

FIGURE 9.1 Hearing and seeing first contact. Photo by Elee Wood.

> I am an object-speaks-for-itself skeptic. Yet in Los Angeles, even though I found problems and difficulties—with a carousel, the lighting, the hard-to-read labels, the overbearing nature of the convention center—I was also drawn to the objects on display. And despite hardened scholarly nerve endings, I was taken by Lincoln's hat. Despite its state of disrepair, its unassuming nature, it was after all Lincoln's hat—the real thing. Then the space suit, the space capsule, Edison's light bulb. All the real stuff. . . . The power of America's Smithsonian was in such epiphanies sparked by individual objects, and in the repeated cumulative effect of the whole. Over and over, visitors were hit with the impact of this experience . . . (p. 37).

Kurin's observation reveals the power of the physical things in the museum. Being in the presence of something perceived as having been a witness to a person or place that is familiar or represents bigger, grander things, can have deeply emotional effects on visitors.

MAXIM 10. Help people reach greater heights.

What can you do help visitors make sense of the ideas or objects? How do you help the visitor navigate the themes of the project through objects? How might this project change someone's life?

The field of education has many theories about how people learn, whether through incremental, step-by-step processes or through holistic, integrated experiences. Whatever orientation you take, one goal for museums is to help people reach greater heights, perhaps through their own knowledge, the inspiration to take action, or feeling connected to their own lives in a deeper way. This might mean helping visitors leave with more information than they came in with. It might mean helping them connect discrete pieces of information with something they already know. It might mean providing them with ways to make a difference, or showing them how to take the idea to the next level. Structuring the experience with objects reinforces visitor success in making connections to the content or the ideas presented in the activity and might just inspire someone along the way.

EXERCISE 19: *"Seeing" What You Know*

Select an object already exhibited at a museum (not the museum with which you are most familiar). Spend 10 minutes looking quietly at the object in context. Then, sit down in front of it and sketch the object for 15 minutes. Don't worry about whether you can draw or not! Draw what you see, understand, or like. Afterwards, while you are still in the presence of the object, close your eyes for five minutes and imagine it. Ask yourself what the object feels like. What does it sound like? After this, quickly jot down a few notes about what was in your mind.

- Compare each of the ways you experienced the object. Was there a difference?
- Did you read the label? If so, at what point? How did that affect your understanding of the object?
- Were there any distractions? What were they? What could you do to counteract them? Or were the distractions useful?
- What did you discover about the object?
- What did you gain from the experience(s)?

WHAT DOES MAXIM 10 LOOK LIKE? Biology Lessons in the Treetops: *Rain Forest,* Milwaukee Public Museum, Milwaukee, Wisconsin. When the exhibit team at Milwaukee Public Museum set out to update their biology hall in the early 1980s, they knew that the exhibit content needed to provide basic information on the principles of modern biology. The museum, well known for its immersive full-scale dioramas, wanted to bring a new level of connection between the exhibit environment and the exhibit content, while at the same time, making it enjoyable. These goals and expectations meant that the exhibition had to serve multiple purposes and meet the needs of many different kinds of visitors.

At the same time that the exhibit team was researching other museums and exhibitions focused on biology, they were aware of the keen public interest around the future of the world's rainforests. By combining the intended content—biology concepts along with an interesting context, the rainforest—the team was able to develop an exhibition experience that provided an extensive base for learning. Visitors could learn about cells and cell biology, biomes, climate, animal and plant behavior, and more. At the same time, the exhibition's emphasis on the rainforest raised issues of deforestation, plant and animal survival, and the need for more research.

In order to help visitors navigate the rainforest exhibit through objects ranging from animal specimens to dioramas and to show scientists at work, the exhibit team needed to provide a rich and detailed visual design. Rather than create the typical diorama the museum uses in other areas of the building, *Rain Forest* incorporates techniques to go further and create a full-fledged immersive environment. The goal throughout the design and planning process was to help visitors feel a strong sense of connection. More importantly, the staff knew that their professional knowledge of the content would be new to most of their visitors. This meant that they had to carefully determine the overarching themes and concepts, and create moments of interaction that enhanced the visitors' experience within the space, motivated them around areas of interest, and sparked an interest in the world around them. By creating content and a design strategy that carefully built visitor knowledge, staff promoted object encounters that helped visitors reach new conclusions about the role of the rainforest and the role of biology as a field of study.

MAXIM 11. **Make it come alive.**

What other formats can help communicate the main ideas? What other ways can you tell the story of the object? How can you help the visitor feel the lives behind this object? How can you help the visitor vividly experience the objects and ideas?

Who wants a dead exhibit? Why do some museums call exhibit labels tombstones? Sadly, rows and rows of objects often have nothing much to say. These dreary and boring (maybe even deadly) moments in the museum are not only design and content issues, but also ones of participation. Making an object come alive in an exhibit or program reinforces the power that objects have in drawing visitors into meaningful, unified experiences in museums.

In the studies we described in Section Two, the multiple experiences people had with objects led to a sense of "actually being there." This perception of shifting across time and space created an energetic, lively feeling of connection with the object. Museum staff can also create moments where the interactions with objects "come alive" in similar ways. Putting the object into a realistic context, a story, program, or dynamic situation can help the visitor think about the object and connect it to new ideas. The visitor can associate the object with various viewpoints that help relate their own experiences with the story and history of the object. In the exercises in this chapter we provide strategies to think about the object in an active environment and to consider the object as an active thing itself rather than lifeless and static. These avenues for participation can build memories and important links to objects that have the power to transform visitor experiences.

EXERCISE 20: *The Talking Pot*

In this exercise, team members help an object to come alive by giving it a voice. The team should sub-divide into several groups, each group choosing a single object from the exhibit script. The subdivided teams will each do a character analysis of their object, developing a persona that they will present to the larger team when done.

- Name the object. Give it an actual name, as if you were naming a pet.
- Decide on its personality. Is it mean, nice, sneaky, smart, young, old, funny?
- What kinds of things does this object like to do? List hobbies, favorite pastimes, favorite food, color, etc.
- In reference to the big idea, write three things this object has to say. Write it in the form of a quote.
- Take a photograph of your object. Print it out. Sketch on the print anything that embellishes the personality of the object.
- When everyone has done this for their objects, introduce your new friend to the rest of the group.

Write a label from the perspective of the object, as if the object were speaking to the viewer. It might be interesting to use one object and have each team member individually and privately write what it has to say, only to share it as a group later. Or, each team member could focus on a different object, so that when sharing the labels in the group part of the session, there is a wider variety of "voices."

WHAT DOES MAXIM 11 LOOK LIKE? **An Object Opera: *The Great Fire Theater,* Museum of History and Industry, Seattle, Washington.** As part of the exhibition, *True Northwest: The Seattle Journey,* visitors can sit in on an object opera that describes the events of the 1889 Great Seattle Fire (Figure 9.2). What is exciting about this moment of object theatre is that rather than being narrated, the presentation features each object as a character in a story—the objects are the actors! They appear in individual cases arranged at the front of a small 40-seat theatre. Behind these objects, historic images and "supertitles" of the lyrics are projected on a large screen.

Each object, from a typewriter to a glue pot, represents a different part of the story. As the narration unfolds, each object "speaks" in first person to provide insight into the events surrounding the fire and its aftermath. When each sings its part at any particular time during the opera, special lighting illuminates it and the other lights are dimmed, just as happens in a real performance. What makes this experience unique beyond the dramatic presentation is that the audience hears the story in a new way, through the "eyes" of the object. When the glue pot, the source of the fire, sings "Don't blame me, it's not my fault," the audience is thrust into a different perspective on the role of objects in this historic event. Similarly while the typewriter and newspaper sing about the news, the audience can follow a slightly different route to see how the story unfolds than just reading about it. What is important about the *Great Fire Theatre* is the use of humor and dramatic tension that help demonstrate each of the characters, bringing the objects to life in a new way. In this instance, while the objects sing for themselves, it all happens through a finely crafted and researched strategy. The voice they take on is one that project developers intended to surprise and delight visitors.

WHAT DOES MAXIM 11 LOOK LIKE? **Tornado Drill: *Weather Permitting,* Minnesota History Center, St. Paul, Minnesota.** The tornado experience in *Weather Permitting,* at the Minnesota History Center is a multimedia presentation that brings to life the intensity of a summer storm. The exterior to the exhibit theatre evokes images of a house turned topsy-turvy by the force of nature. Visitors enter a doorway and find themselves in a re-created 1960s suburban basement, complete with workbench, television set, and radio.

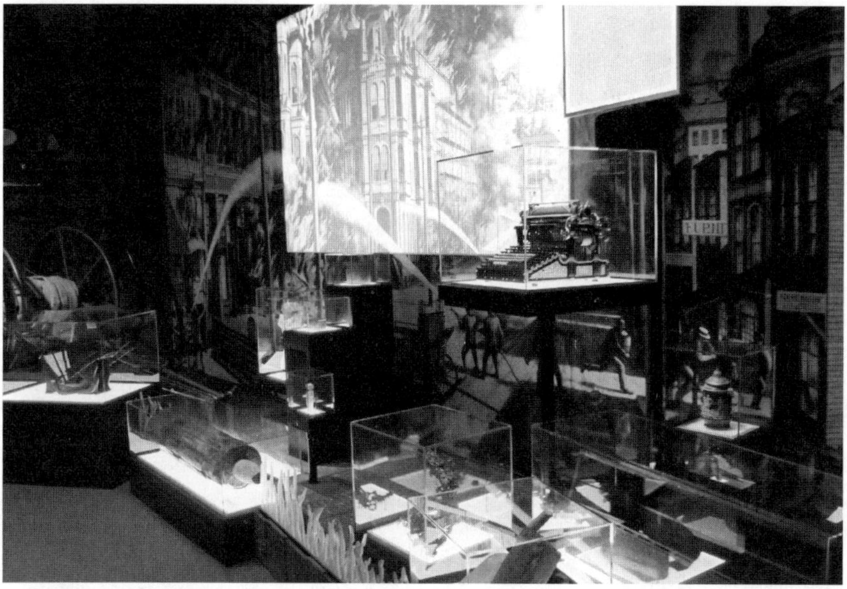

FIGURE 9.2 Objects sing for themselves. Photo by Elee Wood.

As the presentation begins, the television and radio come to life, setting the stage for the moments that happen just before a tornado arrives, putting the visitors into the role of an anxious family sitting in the basement. First comes an announcement to seek shelter, then a siren, then the lights flicker and go dark. As the audience sits in semi-darkness on the cold hard stairs and floor, the basement window provides the only insight to the outside world. Sounds of rain and thunder, vibrations of the wind, flashes of light, then unnerving quiet engulf the space, and a powerful sense of awe, fear, excitement, and wonder sets in. Through the window, an eerie green light emerges slowly as the tornado approaches. For visitors who know life in active tornado country during the summer, the experience is real and vivid. The tornado arrives as rain and hail pelt the windows, the plants outside bend over at the force of the wind, the seats rumble, the wind howls, and then, it's all over. As the storm passes, all becomes quiet; the lights and television slowly come back to life to provide the story of the aftermath. Even the lighting through the window has changed to reveal that the storm has passed. Actual footage of the news from the time explains the feelings and emotions of the real people who went through the experience.

The tornado presentation gives visitors the sense that they are there, in that time and place, sharing a powerfully emotional and even dangerous experience with others. The sensory elements along with the dramatic tension and tales of others make this a vivid experience. The objects included in the Tornado presentation are not necessarily special; instead, they serve to create the setting and context of basements from the time period. The details in the space help provide an important sense of "being there" for visitors, bringing the experience to life.

MAXIM 12. **Start with end in mind.**

Imagine your visitor leaving the exhibit. What are they thinking, feeling, saying? What would you hope for them to think, feel, say? What is the overall result you want when everything is complete? What memories do you want the visitor to have about the objects they have seen?

If you don't know where you want to go with an idea, it doesn't matter what path you choose—you can't get there. Not knowing the goals or purposes of including an object in an experience is not a good way to introduce new ideas or experience to visitors. When a project team starts with the end goals in mind—with a purposeful and intentional use of an object—they can make stronger connections among the content, the design, and the experience of the exhibit. Keeping focused on *why* a team includes an object, not always on *what* objects they include, can provide exciting ways to showcase the messages of the exhibit or program. These exercises will help build stronger and more intentional visitor encounters with objects.

EXERCISE 21: *Envisioning Encounters*

Consider an object for inclusion in an exhibit or project. What role will the object play in the visitor experience? What do you want visitors to do with it once they encounter the object? As a team, make a list of three things it is hoped each object will do as a member of the exhibit.

Think about the role of objects in the visitor's experience:

- How will the visitor see him or herself in the object?
- With what memories about the objects will the visitor have? Will they have any lasting memories of it?
- Will the placement or focus on the object create a memory or evoke a feeling? How will it do that?
- What stories might the visitor retell using the objects?

As the team envisions possible encounters with the object, keep in mind the process that the visitor might take to get to that experience. Be sure to think about how the visitor gets from the starting point of the exhibit to this moment that you've envisioned.

WHAT DOES MAXIM 12 LOOK LIKE? *Sowing Ideas:* Plants are Up to Something, *The Huntington, San Marino, California.* In botanical gardens, plants are the stars of the show. Even so, as living and growing things, their presence, even in a botanical garden, can sometimes be taken for granted. In *Plants are Up to Something* at the Huntington Library and Botanical Gardens in San Marino, California, the actual process of how plants live comes to the foreground. The sometimes slow and undetectable elements of plants' lives become part of the Gardens' main message of plant diversity and activity. Visitors have the opportunity to explore the wide range of plant anatomy, and develop their awareness of plant habitats and the need for habitat conservation.

It is the "secrets" of plant activity, made plain and clear for the visitor to investigate, that are the end results of the exhibit. People like to find out the inside story that each of the plants in the exhibit contains. Labels connect plant activity to elements of human life in order to make the concepts easier to understand. The secrets of plant processes are relatable and help all kinds of visitors make sense of the information. In an activity on pitcher plants, visitors investigate plant digestion by sorting through the corpses of the dead bugs and insects inside the plant. Labels and hands-on experiences give visitors the chance to simulate a variety of plant processes. Multiple sensory elements help visitors see, hear, and smell plants up close and in incredible detail. What's more, the use of beautiful, unusual, and intriguing plants draws visitors in for a closer look. Using real plants reinforces many ideas about the care for plants, as well as the fragile nature of all living things. By exploring principles of botany through the real things, visitors are better able to make connections to the world of plants than they might were it a model. Similarly, the presence of real tools and equipment, and the encouragement to practice science skills, fosters active experimentation by visitors. By the end, visitors leave feeling as if they have unlocked the mysteries of the world of plants.

EXERCISE 22: *Object Hopscotch*

In this exercise the goal is to imagine the links and connections between objects in the exhibit and the visitor takeaway messages. Imagine a hopscotch game where the end result is the "home space" and each of the squares on the court are one of the objects in the exhibit. For each object in the hopscotch game, list all of the possible connections (you can even draw a hopscotch game on the ground if you want) that the object has with the ones that surround it. Create a narrative that allows the player to get from the home space through all of the hopscotch squares and back again. This process can help you see how well each object connects the others and how easily a visitor can make connections between them.

WHAT DOES MAXIM 12 LOOK LIKE? Connecting Content: *Dancing Shadows, Epic Tales: Wayang Kulit of Indonesia,* Museum of International Folk Art, Santa Fe, New Mexico. Representing the diverse cultures of the world through folk art is part of the mission of the Museum of International Folk Art, in Santa Fe, New Mexico. In the exhibition, *Dancing Shadows, Epic Tales: Wayang Kulit of Indonesia,* a primary goal was to introduce the complexity of Indonesian culture through the objects of *wayang kulit,* an intricate and detailed performance art form that includes shadow puppets, music, and storytelling.

To help museum audiences see the links between culture and art, the goal for this exhibition was to develop a rich experience that would provide visitors with a deeper understanding of the nuances of the *wayang kulit* form. To do this they developed experiences that helped visitors appreciate the process of presenting the traditional stories, and in experiencing the stories as the viewer. Among the many key elements of the exhibition was a puppet stage that visitors could view from both the front and back. The exhibition team achieved these viewpoints by projecting video of front and back views of a performance. These images worked in conjunction to give an accurate sense of how an audience might view, and how a performer might see, the overall production.

The team's intent to share the complexity of the *wayang kulit* experience as an example of Indonesian culture meant the exhibition expressed the same cultural concepts in multiple formats throughout, supporting the visitor experience by creating a layered set of messages. For example, the names of the puppet types and characters were constantly and consistently repeated throughout the exhibition. The visitor could make connections to cultural messages across the many exhibit components, and could gain perspective by delving deeply into just one of the elements of the exhibition. As a result, visitors were able to live *through* the experience of the puppet show in ways that helped them build a respect for Indonesian culture.

WHAT DOES MAXIM 12 LOOK LIKE? Inside and Behind the Scenes: *Cocoon*, The Darwin Centre, Natural History Museum, London, England
An excellent example of starting with the end in mind is the new Darwin Centre at London's Natural History Museum (NMH). Opened in 2009, and built with the intent to share—or perhaps redefine—the behind-the-scenes activities of a museum with its public, *Cocoon* is a seven story, organic, oval structure, built to house the museum's 20 million specimens. It is surrounded by a glass and steel structure that holds state of the art scientific research facilities. Hundreds of museum scientists work here, and the structure provides access (in multiple ways) to every curve of the unique edifice.

Surrounding *Cocoon* is a winding angled pathway, moving up all the way to the top of the building. Along the way are windows into the storage area, as well as stations that invite visitors to find out what goes on inside the research facility. There are various viewing windows into the collection storage space and the spaces where specimens are prepared. Visitors can even ask working scientists questions about their activity using an intercom system.

From the beginning, the project's goal was to allow the public to interact with the museum's researchers. Visitors get an insight into their daily work, whether it's collecting and naming new species or organizing collections that help study current issues such as climate change or diseases like malaria. Every activity on the route up *Cocoon* is meant to connect the visitor to the objects and the people that care for them, and ultimately to give the public a sense of ownership over the environment of the world.

Transformation through Participation Takeaways

If objects are to be a primary tool for powerful experiences in the museum, then giving the public greater access to those objects, on multiple levels, becomes an important goal for all museum staff. Visitors' direct contact with the object, through participatory experiences and experiences that evoke strong emotions and connections, is what helps to transform the meaning of the object. Participatory experiences in museums build greater connection between the objectworld and the visitor's lifeworld. The closer these two worlds come together, and ultimately overlap, the more opportunity there is for a unified experience.

Museum staff help promote more meaningful visitor-object encounters by working through intentional processes to establish the goals and use of objects in an exhibit. Similarly, by bringing the objects to life through vivid presentations and displays, staff highlight the objectworld in new ways. Structuring the information and organizing participatory experiences with objects helps all visitors make personal connections to the object and feel successful as a result. Combining the goals for the visitor with real, tangible physical objects further reinforces the power that objects have to bring ideas into the emotional world of visitors, which in turn helps them connect, explore, and wonder about the world around them. The transformation of objects into these participatory experiences will ultimately lead to deeper meaning and interest in the experiences the museum presents and create lasting memories for visitors.

CHAPTER TEN

The End is the Beginning

For some, the ideas we've presented thus far will be new orientations to years-old practices. For others, they may give permission to do something different or exciting with objects. Still others, already applying similar principles, may feel a sigh of relief: at last, someone else understands the significance of people's experiences with objects! Moving ahead with the ideas presented here is about reclaiming a museum's role in providing unique and compelling encounters with *objects*. As we have argued, those objects are not just artifacts, specimens, and artwork; they are the tangible things that constitute the world around us. Making this subtle shift in the definition of objects and the conception of how museum collections connect to visitors, of how people come to "know" objects, is a critical component of successful museum experiences.

The Object Knowledge Framework promotes a different way of knowing objects through more than just their factual details. Instead, it focuses on ways that people use objects to shape and make sense of their world. The coupling of person and object *together* in the museum experience involves respect for a museum visitor's lifeworld, the unique perspective on experiences and ways of knowing that each person has. Object meanings are not static records or entries in a database: rather they are the infinite meanings brought to each object by everyone who has ever encountered it, before or during its life in a museum.

A visitor-object encounter in the museum arises when museum staff members work together in a networked system of object care, design, content development, educational experiences, marketing, and beyond. Each member of a museum team brings different kinds of object knowledge and experience, and this expertise is essential not only in opening a wide door for interpretation of information, but also in the transformation of

Elizabeth Wood and Kiersten F. Latham, "The End is the Beginning" in *The Objects of Experience: Transforming Visitor-Object Encounters in Museums*, pp 163-166.

objects that supports the distinctive kind of connections that museums provide visitors.

Putting all of these ideas about objects into play in museum projects requires museum staff to think differently about objects. Through the process of using the Framework in museum planning, teams can constantly involve and integrate the multiple meaning of objects gathered through visitor research and reflection by the team. Without question, museum planning teams already oversee a wide variety of details related to using objects in exhibitions and programs. Care of the museum's collection is paramount, but visitor access, fidelity of information, and overall appeal are equally important for a successful visitor experience. We hope that, through this book, teams can draw on the Object Knowledge Framework to augment and shape their planning—but we don't expect that this kind of change will be easy for everyone. We offer three entryways into using the Framework: philosophically, practically, and personally.

Philosophically

Being able to articulate a personal philosophy about objects is a great place to reflect on how the Object Knowledge Framework fits into museum practice. Take, for example, each component of the Framework. How do the ideas of the lifeworld, the objectworld, and the unified experience play out in the museum setting? Do some parts make more sense than others? How do you understand the interplay between the individual, group, and material dimensions? How do these concepts apply to the world beyond the museum?

Experience and prior knowledge in the field shape practice, and in some cases not all of the material presented here will relate to the reader's own experience. However, the examples and details about the maxims may be useful guides for thinking about why these strategies work in some museum settings. The Framework (or parts of it) could be used to bring together staff with diverse backgrounds to help everyone "get on the same page" or to forge a team-wide or museum-wide philosophy about what objects mean or how the museum wants to position them in achieving its mission.

Another strategy for using this book philosophically is to go beyond the book itself and examine the research findings that feed the model. These ideas reiterate the role that objects play across the range of human experience. Perhaps there's an opportunity to conduct your own visitor research using the Framework or ideas from influential thinkers behind it. Gathering ideas about what might work, how it could happen, and why it matters to the museum are strong approaches to build advocacy for the visitor-object encounter in the museum.

Practically

Practical implementation of the Object Knowledge Framework might begin with creating a reading group and discussion on how to institute the maxims into existing processes. Teams can use the exercises as part of planning meetings. Applying these ideas to new projects as they come about will provide a useful comparison with existing projects. The Framework even presents an opportunity to evaluate current exhibits and programs to see how well the ideas of visitor-object encounters are integrated.

Starting on a small scale and slowly incorporating these tactics into planning might be a good way to test out which ideas resonate with planning teams. Others might think about where these ideas apply beyond exhibits and programs, and how they might work in other areas of the museum. Gathering members from across the museum's areas of responsibility and discussing the concepts helps others think about how the Framework makes sense in their work. Take these ideas and make them yours. Adjust them to make them fit your institution.

Personally

Personal investigation of the Object Knowledge Framework might be the easiest way to start. It could start with making an inventory of your personal objects and considering what they mean to you. It could involve a reflection on moments of unified experience (and whether you have had these) and where they happened, what they looked like, and who was there. From here, taking these memories and emotions related to your own private objects into professional work aids in promoting advocacy for the role of objects within the museum experience. Drawing on the ideas of integration, network, and connection could lead to new discoveries about the way that objects unite people and identity. When you visit other museums, look for elements of the Framework, which maxims are in play, and how these museums encourage individual experience with objects. All of these personal efforts to become better connected to the objectworld and to see things through the filters of the lifeworld will undoubtedly provide new perspectives and excitement for your work.

What is most important about the Object Knowledge Framework is that it provides a fresh way to look at and think about the meaning of objects in human life. The ideas in this book are here for the reader to take them and make them their own and, ultimately, bring that approach to museum work. Just as the maxim suggests, “Leave room for more,” this book itself is an object that you can process through the material, group, and individual ways of knowing, each influencing your personal connection to the content. Objects have many meanings; so too does this model for thinking about the role of objects in the visitor experience.

REFERENCES

Adair, B., Filene, B., & Koloski, L. (Eds.). (2011). Letting go? Sharing historical authority in a user-generated world. Philadelphia, PA: Pew Center for Arts & Heritage.

American Museum of Natural History. (2012). Dance and Belief [Exhibit].

American Museum of Natural History. (2013). "The Spectrum of Life." www.amnh.org/exhibitions/permanent-exhibitions/biodiversity-and-environmental-halls/hall-of-biodiversity/the-spectrum-of-life (Accessed January 12, 2013).

Ayto, J. (1990). *Dictionary of word origins.* New York: Arcade.

Bachelard, G. (1968). *The poetics of space* (M. Jolas, Trans.). Boston, MA: Beacon.

Bourcier, P., & Rogers, R. (Eds.). (2010). *Nomenclature for museum cataloging, 3.0.* Lanham, MD: AltaMira Press.

Briet, S. (2006). *What is documentation? English translation of the classic French text* (R. E. Day & L. Martinet, Trans.). Lanham, MD: Scarecrow Press, Inc.

Buckland, M. (1991). Information as thing. *Journal of the American Society for Information Science, 42*(5): 351-360.

Buckland, M. (1998). What is a "document"? In T. B. Hahn & M. Buckland (Eds.), *Historical Studies in Information Science* (pp. 220). Medford, NJ: Information Today.

Cameron, C. M., & Gatewood, J. B. (2000). Excursions into the un-remembered past: What people want from visits to historical sites. *The Public Historian, 22*(3), 107–127.

Cameron, C. M., & Gatewood, J. B. (2003). Seeking numinous experiences in the unremembered past. *Ethnology, 42*(1), 55–71.

Candlin, F., & Guins, R. (2009). *The object reader.* London, England: Routledge.

Caple, C. (2006). *Objects.* Hoboken, NJ: Taylor & Francis.

Chatterjee, H., MacDonald, S., Prytherch, D., & Noble, G. (2008). *Touch in museums: Policy and practice in object handling.* Oxford, England: Berg.

Conn, S. (1998). *Museums and American intellectual life, 1876-1826.* Chicago: University of Chicago.

Conn, S. (2010). *Do museums still need objects?* Philadelphia, PA: University of Pennsylvania Press.

Csíkszentmihalyi, M. (1990). *Flow: The psychology of optimal experience.* New York, NY: HarperCollins.

Csíkszentmihalyi, M., & Rochberg-Halton, E. (1981). *The meaning of things: Domestic symbols and the self.* Cambridge, England: Cambridge University Press.

de Guzman, R. (2010). Getting over it. In B. Henry & K. McLean (Eds.), *How visitors changed our museum* (pp. 88-89). Oakland, CA: Oakland Museum of California.

Dewey, J. (1916). *Democracy and education: An introduction to the philosophy of education.* New York: Free Press.

Dewey, J. (1934). *Art as experience.* New York: Perigree.

Dewey, J., & Bentley, A. F. (1949). *Knowing and the known.* Boston, MA: Beacon Press.

Doering, Z. D., & Pekarik, A. J. (1996). Questioning the entrance narrative. *Journal of Museum Education 21*(3), 20-23.
Dudley, S. (2010). *Museum materialities: Objects, engagements, interpretations.* London, England: Routledge.
Duensing, S. (2002). The object of experience. In S. Paris (Ed.), *Perspectives on object-centered learning in museums* (pp. 317-328). Mahwah, NJ: Lawrence Erlbaum.
Empathy. *Glossary of literary terms.* Gale Cengage Learning. www.gale.cengage.com/free_resources/glossary/index.htm (Accessed June 2, 2013)
Evans, E. M., Mull, M. S., & Poling, D. A. (2002). The authentic object? A child's-eye view. In S. Paris (Ed.), *Perspectives on object-centered learning in museums* (pp. 50-71). Mahwah, NJ: Lawrence Erlbaum.
Falk, J. H., & Dierking, L. D. (1992). *The museum experience.* Washington, DC: Whalesback Books.
Falk, J. H., & Dierking, L. D. (2000). *Learning from museums: Visitor experiences and the making of meaning.* Lanham, MD: AltaMira Press.
Filene, B. (2011). Make yourself at home—welcoming voices in open house: If these walls could talk. In B. Adair, B. Filene, & L. Koloski (Eds.), *Letting go? Sharing historical authority in a user-generated world* (pp. 138-155). Philadelphia, PA: Pew Center for Arts & Heritage.
Fleming, E. M. (1974). Artifact study: A proposed model. *Winterthur Portfolio 9,* 153-173.
Gatewood, J. B., & Cameron, C. M. (2004). Battlefield pilgrims at Gettysburg National Military Park. *Ethnology, 43*(3), 193–216.
Gordon, T. S. (2012). *Private history in public: Exhibition and the settings of everyday life.* Lanham, MD: AltaMira Press.
Graburn, N. (1977). The museum and the visitor experience. In L. Draper (Ed.), *The visitor and the museum* (pp. 5-26). Seattle, WA: Museum Educators of the American Association of Museums.
Gurian, E. H. (2006). What is the object of this exercise? In *Civilizing the museum: The collected works of Elaine Heumann Gurian* (pp. 33-47). [Original published 1999] London, England: Routledge.
Harman, G. (2011). *The quadruple object.* Arlesfort, England: Zero Books.
Heidegger, M. (1967). *What is a thing?* (W.B. Barton & V. Deutsch, Trans.). Chicago, IL: Henry Regnery.
Hein, H. (2000). *The museum in transition: A philosophical perspective.* Washington, DC: Smithsonian Institution Press.
Henry, B., & McLean, K. (2010). *How visitors changed our museum: Transforming the Gallery of California Art at the Oakland Museum of California.* Oakland, CA: Oakland Museum of California.
Hirasuna, D. (2005). *The art of gaman: Arts and crafts from the Japanese American internment camps 1942-1946.* Berkeley, CA: Ten Speed Press.
Hodder, I. (1986). *Reading the past: Current approaches to interpretation in archaeology.* Cambridge, England: Cambridge University Press.
Hood, M. (2004). Why people choose not to visit museums. In G. Anderson (Ed.), *Reinventing the museum: Historical and contemporary perspectives on the paradigm shift* (pp. 150-157). Walnut Creek, CA: AltaMira Press.

Hood, B. & Santos, L. (Eds.). (2009). *The origins of object knowledge.* Oxford, England: Oxford University Press.

Hooper-Greenhill, E. (1992). *Museums and the shaping of knowledge.* London: Routledge.

Hooper-Greenhill, E. (2000). *Museums and the interpretation of visual culture.* London, England: Routledge.

Hoskins, J. (1998). *Biographical objects: How things tell the stories of people's lives.* New York, NY: Routledge.

Hudson, K. (1977). *Museums for the 1980s: A survey of world trends.* New York, NY: Holmes & Meier Publishers.

Indianapolis Museum of Art. (2012). *Ere ibeji (Twin male figure).* [Gallery label.] www.imamuseum.org/collections/artwork/female-twin-figure-ere-ibeji (Accessed Sept 30, 2012)

International Committee on Museology. (2009). *Museology: Back to basics. ICOFOM Study Series 38.* Vevey, Switzerland: International Committee for Museology.

Kari, J. & Hartel, J. (2007). Information and higher things in life: Addressing the pleasurable and the profound in information science. *Journal of the American Society for Information Science and Technology, 58*(8), 1131-1147.

Knappert, C. (2005).*Thinking through material culture: An interdisciplinary perspective.* Philadelphia, PA: University of Pennsylvania.

Korn, R. (2004). Self-portrait: First know thyself, then serve your public. *Museum News,* January/February, 32-35, 50-52.

Kurin, R. (1997). From Smithsonian's America to America's Smithsonian. *Museum Anthropology 21*(1), 27-41.

Latham, K. F. (2007). The poetry of the museum: A holistic model of numinous museum experiences. *Museum Management and Curatorship, 22*(3), 247-263.

Latham, K. F. (2009). *Numinous experiences with museum objects* (unpublished doctoral dissertation). Emporia State University, Emporia, KS.

Leinhardt, G. & Crowley, K. (2002). Objects of learning, objects of talk: Changing minds in museums. In S. Paris (Ed), *Perspectives on object-centered learning in museums* (pp. 301-324). Mahwah, NJ: Lawrence Erlbaum.

Lopez, D. S. (1979). Approaching the numinous: Rudolph Otto and Tibetan tantra. *Philosophy East and West 2,* 465-476.

Lund, N. W. (2004). Documentation in a complementary perspective. In W. B. Rayward (Ed.), *Aware and responsible!:Papers of the 2001 Nordic-International Colloquium on Social and Cultural Awareness and Responsibility in Library, Information and Documentation Studies* (SCARLID) (pp. 93-102). Lanham, MD: Scarecrow Press.

Maeda, J. (2006). *The laws of simplicity: Design, technology, business, life.* Cambridge, MA: MIT Press.

Marcoux, J. S. (2001). The refurbishment of memory. In D. Miller (Ed.), *Home possessions: Material culture behind closed doors* (pp. 69-86). Oxford, England: Berg.

Maroevic, I. (1991).The exhibition as presentative communication. In H. K. Vieregg & A. B. Shah (Eds.). *The language of exhibitions: ICOM International Committee for Museology Study Series.* Vevey, Switzerland: International Committee for Museology.

McLean, K. (1993). *Planning for people in museum exhibitions.* Washington, DC: Association of Science-Technology Centers.

Mezirow, J. (Ed.). (2000). *Learning as transformation: Critical perspectives on a theory in progress*. San Francisco, CA: Jossey-Bass.

Milwaukee Public Museum. (2007). *Samson & Sambo, Simba & Timba: Behind the dioramas*. Milwaukee, WI: Milwaukee Public Museum.

Mitten, D. (2007). The axe head. In S. Turkle (Ed.), *Evocative objects: Things we think with* (pp. 118-125). Cambridge, MA: MIT Press.

Neumeier. (2009). *The designful company: How to build a culture of nonstop innovation*. Berkeley, CA: New Riders.

Oakland Museum of California. (2012).*Top 100: Faces of change*. [Exhibit label]. Oakland, CA: Oakland Museum of California.

Ohio Historical Society. (2013). *Controversy: Pieces you don't normally see*. [Promotional materials]. Columbus, OH: Ohio Historical Society.

Olsen, B. (2010). *In defense of things: Archaeology and the ontology of objects*. Lanham, MD: AltaMira.

Otto, R. (1965). *The idea of the holy: An inquiry into the non-rational factor in the idea of the divine and its relation to the rational* (J. W. Harvey, Trans.) [Original work published 1917]. London, England: Oxford University Press.

Oxford English dictionary (2nd ed.). (1989). New York, NY: Oxford University Press.

Object Stories. (2011a). "Ancestral Knowledge Roots us to Home. Dena Dartt-Newton." Portland Art Museum. objectstories.org/stories/#!/?Story=ce96b03a-8156-e111-a81d-001ec9bb218f (Accessed November 11, 2012)

Object Stories. (2011b). "This is so cool, so sweet. Ted Smith." Portland Art Museum. objectstories.org/stories/#!/?Story=20780a55-5b4a-e011-abac-001ec9bb218f (Accessed November 11, 2012)

Object Stories. (2011c). "How to Tell Your Story." Portland Art Museum. objectstories.org/faq/index.html (Accessed November 11, 2012)

Pearce, S. (Ed.). (1990). *Objects of knowledge*. London: The Athlone Press.

Pearce, S. (1994). Interpreting objects and collections. London: Routledge.

Peirce, C. S. (1934). Collected papers: Volume V. Pragmatism and pragmaticism. Cambridge, MA: Harvard University Press.

Pine, B. J., & Gilmore, J. H. (1999). *The experience economy*. Boston: Harvard Business School Press.

Pitt Rivers Museum. (2012). "Research Introduction." University of Oxford. www.prm.ox.ac.uk/researchintro.html (Accessed January 20, 2013)

Prentice, R. C., Witt, S. F., & Hamer, C. (1998). Tourism as experience: The case of heritage parks. *Annals of Tourism Research, 25*(1), 1-24.

Prown, J. (1982). Mind in matter: An introduction to material culture theory and method. *Winterthur Portfolio, 17*(1), 1-19.

Pye, E. (2007). *The power of touch: Handling objects in museum and heritage contexts*. Walnut Creek, CA: Left Coast Press, Inc.

Roberts, L. C. (1997). *From knowledge to narrative: Educators and the changing museum*. Washington, DC: Smithsonian Institution Press.

Rosenblatt, L. M. (1978). *The reader, the text, the poem: The transactional theory of the literary work*. Carbondale, IL: Southern Illinois University Press.

Rothstein, E. (2011, June 22). Where park visitors answer a call to battle. *The New York Times*, p C2.

Schlereth, T. J. (1992). Object knowledge: Every museum visitor an interpreter. In *Patterns in practice: Selections from the Journal of Museum Education* (pp.102-111). Washington, DC: Museum Education Roundtable.

Serrell, B. (1996). Exhibit labels: An interpretive approach. Walnut Creek, CA: AltaMira Press.

Silverman, L. H. (2002). Taking a wider view of museum outcomes and experiences: Theory, research and magic. *Journal of Education in Museums, 23*, 3-8.

Spock, M. (2000). When I grow up I'd like to work in a place like this. *Curator: The Museum Journal, 43*(1), 19-32.

Taborsky, E. (1990). The discursive object. In S. Pearce (Ed.), *Objects of knowledge* (pp. 50-77). London, England: The Athlone Press.

Tilden, F. (1957). *Interpreting our heritage: Principles and practices for visitor services in parks, museums, and historic places.* Chapel Hill, NC: University of North Carolina Press.

Trustees of the British Museum. (2013). "Telling the human story of Pompeii and Herculaneum." blog post by Vanessa Baldwin, exhibition project curator. blog.britishmuseum.org/2013/03/28/telling-the-human-story-of-pompeii-and-herculaneum/ (Accessed April 10, 2013).

Turkle, S. (2007). *Evocative objects: Things we think with*. Cambridge, MA: MIT Press.

Verghese, A. (2012, October 9). The doctor's bag for the new millennium. *The New York Times*, p. D2.

Watt, M. K. (2011). "Blanket Stories: Objects." hmkwatt.com/index.php/content/work_detail/category/blanket_stories_objects/ (Accessed June 12, 2013)

Wehner, K., & Sear, M. (2010). Engaging the material world: Object knowledge and Australian journeys. In S. Dudley (Ed.), *Museum materialities: Objects, engagements, interpretations (pp. 143-161)*. London, England: Routledge.

Wertsch, J. (2002). Epistemological issues about objects. In S. Paris (Ed.), *Perspectives on object-centered learning in museums* (pp. 102-108). Mahwah, NJ: Lawrence Erlbaum.

Wood, E. (2005). *Objects matter: The meaning of objects from childhood.* (Unpublished doctoral dissertation). University of Minnesota, Minneapolis, MN.

Wood, E. (2009). Rules for the (R)evolution of Museums. In *Inspiring Action: Museums and Social Change* (pp. 22-38). Edinburgh: Museums Etc.

Wood, E., & Latham, K. F. (2009). Object knowledge: Researching objects in the museum experience. *Reconstruction: Studies in Contemporary Culture, 9*(1). reconstruction.eserver.org/091/wood&latham.shtml (Accessed June 10, 2101)

Wood, E. & Latham, K. F. (2011). The Thickness of the Things: Exploring the Museum Curriculum through Phenomenological Touch. *Journal of Curriculum Theorizing, 27*(2): 51-65.

INDEX

Page numbers in italics page refer to illustrations.

ABOUT THE AUTHORS

Elizabeth (Elee) Wood is an associate professor at Indiana University-Purdue University Indianapolis. She serves as the director of the Museum Studies program, IU School of Liberal Arts, and holds a joint appointment in Education, IU School of Education, and as public scholar of museums, families, and learning in-residence at the internationally renowned Children's Museum of Indianapolis. Her research interests include object-based learning, informal learning in community settings, and critical museum pedagogies. Wood teaches courses in Museum Education, Museums and Audiences, Museum Theatre, and Object-Based Learning. She has presented on the concepts of object knowledge and biographical objects both nationally and internationally at conferences on museums, material culture, and qualitative research. Elee got her museum start early as a youth interpreter in the Wizard Wing at the Milwaukee Public Museum and worked as a museum exhibit developer, program manager, and evaluator.

Kiersten F. Latham is an assistant professor in the School of Library and Information Science at Kent State University, where she created and teaches the museum studies specialization within the MLIS program. Some courses she teaches include Foundations of Museum Studies, Museum Communication, Museum Collections, Museum Users, The Museum System, Museum Origins, and Material Culture and Meaning. In addition to academic work, she has practiced in museums in various positions from collection manager and curator to living history interpreter for over 20 years. Her research interests focus on the meaning of museum objects, especially with respect to emotion, perception, sensation, and spirituality. Presently, she is studying the meaning of materiality to museum users. She has done research on numinous experiences with museum objects, phenomenological touch (of museum objects), and conceptual ramifications of museum object as document, following the ideas of Michael Buckland and Suzanne Briet.

Wood and Latham have been collaborating on object-based thinking in museums since 2006. Together they have published two articles, "Object Knowledge: Using Phenomenology in Object Research and Museum Experiences"—the theoretical basis for this book—and "The Thickness of Things: Exploring the Curriculum of Museums through Phenomenological Touch"—an expanded investigation of objects and touch in museum settings. In addition, Wood and Latham have presented internationally, two such presentations being *Exploring the Phenomenon of Representation, Identity,* and *Experience through Object Knowledge and Intertwining Body/Self/Museum.* In addition to academic conferences, they regularly present at the American Association Museums conference; past presentations include *Beyond Hands-On, The Secret Life of Objects* and *Is the Object Experience?* (with Andrew Pekarik).